the
Unofficial
Guide® to
Branson, Missouri
3rd Edition

Also available from IDG Books Worldwide, Inc.

Beyond Disney: The Unofficial Guide to Universal, Sea World, and the Best of Central Florida, by Bob Sehlinger and Amber Morris

Inside Disney: The Incredible Story of Walt Disney World and the Man Behind the Mouse, by Eve Zibart

Mini Las Vegas: The Pocket-Sized Unofficial Guide, by Bob Sehlinger

Mini-Mickey: The Pocket-Sized Unofficial Guide to Walt Disney World, by Bob Sehlinger

The Unofficial Guide to Bed & Breakfasts in California, by Mary Anne Moore and Maurice Read

The Unofficial Guide to Bed & Breakfasts in New England, by Lea Lane

The Unofficial Guide to Bed & Breakfasts in the Northwest, by Sally O'Neal Coates

The Unofficial Guide to California with Kids, by Colleen Dunn Bates and Susan LaTempa

The Unofficial Guide to Chicago, by Joe Surkiewicz and Bob Sehlinger

The Unofficial Guide to Cruises, by Kay Showker with Bob Sehlinger

The Unofficial Guide to Disneyland, by Bob Sehlinger

The Unofficial Guide to Florida with Kids, by Pam Brandon

The Unofficial Guide to Golf Vacatioins in the Eastern U.S., by Joseph Mark Passov with C. H. Conroy

The Unofficial Guide to the Great Smoky and Blue Ridge Region, by Bob Sehlinger and Joe Surkiewicz

The Unofficial Guide to Hawaii, by Lance Tominaga

The Unofficial Guide to Las Vegas, by Bob Sehlinger

The Unofficial Guide to London, by Lesley Logan

The Unofficial Guide to Miami and the Keys, by Bob Sehlinger and Joe Surkiewicz

The Unofficial Guide to New York City, by Eve Zibart and Bob Sehlinger with Jim Leff and Lea Lane

The Unofficial Guide to New Orleans, by Bob Sehlinger and Eve Zibart

The Unofficial Guide to Paris, by David Applefield

The Unofficial Guide to San Francisco, by Joe Surkiewicz and Bob Sehlinger with Richard Sterling

The Unofficial Guide to Skiing in the West, by Lito Tejada-Flores, Peter Shelton, Seth Masia, Ed Chauner, and Bob Sehlinger

The Unofficial Guide to Walt Disney World, by Bob Sehlinger

The Unofficial Guide to Walt Disney World for Grown-Ups, by Eve Zibart

The Unofficial Guide to Walt Disney World with Kids, by Bob Sehlinger

The Unofficial Guide to Washington, D.C., by Bob Sehlinger and Joe Surkiewicz with Eve Zibart

the Unofficial Guide® to Branson, Missouri

3rd Edition

Eve Zibart
with Bob Sehlinger

For Sandy Liles, without whom this book might have been possible, but not fun.
—E. Z.

Every effort has been made to ensure the accuracy of information throughout this book. Bear in mind, however, that prices, schedules, etc., are constantly changing. Readers should always verify information before making final plans.

IDG Books Worldwide, Inc.
An International Data Group Company
919 E. Hillsdale Blvd., Suite 400
Foster City, CA 94404

Copyright © 2000 by Bob Sehlinger
3rd edition

Produced by Menasha Ridge Press

ISBN 0-02-863800X

ISSN 1097-1580

Manufactured in the United States of America

10 9 8 7 6 5 4 3 2 1

Contents

6 Theme Parks, Museums, and Other Attractions

7 Restaurants and Dining

8 Shopping

9 Outdoor Recreation

List of Maps

Acknowledgments

Nearly everyone in Branson was extremely helpful, but a few people went out of their ways to offer tips, advice, and guidance (or just a drink). Special thanks to Dan Lennon of the Lawrence Welk group and "Mustang Steve" at the Osmond Family Theatre.

And as always, thanks to Bob and the Doc, Grant, Shannon, Molly, Georgia, Annie, Steve, and Clay.

—Eve Zibart

the Unofficial Guide® to Branson, Missouri

3rd Edition

Introduction

Introducing . . . Branson, Missouri!

WHAT IS BRANSON, ANYWAY?

If you've only recently heard of Branson, Missouri, you shouldn't feel silly. It is still in many ways a boomtown—with some of the growing pains that implies—and in terms of vacation spots, something of a newcomer. But don't expect a sleepy Ozarks resort town: Depending on which figures you use, Branson is either the leading or the number two drive-to destination in the United States, with Disney World the other giant. Over six million-plus tourists visited Branson in 1997; with its original seven-month "season" rapidly expanding into 10 and even 12 months a year, it can only get busier.

So what is Branson? For starters, it's the self-proclaimed "Live Entertainment Capital" of the country, a PG-rated cross between Nashville and Las Vegas. It's wall-to-wall performances, two or three times a day (or even more). More specifically, it's a celebration of country and pop music that fills three dozen theaters, outlet shopping malls, three theme parks, several museums, and paddle-wheelers, with more of each of the above under construction.

It's also an outdoor recreation mecca, with three lakes, record-breaking trout and bass fishing, golf courses, camping, and water sports. And all pretty much within an area eight miles square.

Branson is the permanent residence of Andy Williams, Mel Tillis, Mickey Gilley, Bobby Vinton, Jim Stafford, Tony Orlando, Yakov Smirnoff, Moe Bandy, 27 members of the Lennon family, and 43 Osmonds. Kenny Rogers and Barbara Mandrell are regulars here and Christy Lane, The Platters, Jennifer Wilson, The Duttons, and Barbara Fairchild are also established attractions, along with such old-fashioned Opry-style variety shows as the *Presleys' Country Jubilee* and *Baldknobbers*

Jamboree. There are even Vegas-style imports: a "waltzing waters" exhibit, magician Kirby Van Burch, and the production shows *Country Tonite!* and *Legends in Concert.*

But Branson isn't just an after-dark phenomenon. If you really want to get your visit's worth, you could, in a single day, see Buck Trent over breakfast and Jim Owen at 10, be in the audience of a live radio broadcast over lunch, dance to Lawrence Welk videos before seeing the show at 2, take an early dinner cruise at 5, and, if you were still hungry, enjoy the Platters while you eat a slab of prime rib. Meanwhile, the kids could be swimming, bungee-jumping, putt-putting, or spending a rainy day at the Ripley's Believe It or Not! Museum.

Which brings us to a little bit of . . .

WHAT BRANSON IS NOT

Branson is not, to be frank, a typical baby-boomer place. Its amusement parks in particular are a good value for families, and some of its variety and production shows will also please parents with kids. There are fewer big draws for singles or for dinks ("dual income, no kids" couples) between 23 and 35, whose favorite country stars are those currently on the charts and video channels, or whose tastes run to more contemporary rock, jazz, Miami pop, or blues. For the same reasons, if your kids are in their middle to late teens, they may not find quite as much to their taste: no hip-hop (with the occasional and brief exception of the Osmonds' Second Generation quartet) and absolutely no rap, no house, no dancehall, no rave or techno, no ambient or alternative rock. (If you've never heard of these last musical genres, you're probably safe in Branson.)

Likewise, there is little for young urbanites accustomed to late-night or "adult" entertainment; many restaurants close down after curtain time, and even some of the hotel dining rooms have limited hours. It's not a big sports town, not a news junkies' town, nor is it particularly upscale in its attractions. There is no gambling—in fact, many of the local performers have been preemptively lobbying the state government *against* legalized gaming. Local police keep an eye on dance bars where broken hips are more common than broken hearts. Alcohol is served in only a very few venues; even the Dixie Belle Saloon at the Dixie Stampede, despite its name, does not serve spirits.

Dining choices are fairly limited. Although we've picked out a dozen or so of the best restaurants in town and profiled them in "Part 7: Restaurants and Dining," there is nothing that could be described as real ethnic or nouvelle cuisine. The four basic food groups in Branson, so to speak, are Tex-Mex, barbecue, prime rib, and buffet—all of which can be very good—but the Midwestern setting is worth remembering if you have special nutritional or dietary requirements.

Branson is, after all, a gathering spot for performers who are no longer, by definition, "on the road." This is fine for them—Andy Williams, for instance, has described his life in Branson as an idyllic round of morning golf, two performances, and an early bedtime, plus, one would imagine, good security—but most of the Branson performers have stopped recording new albums or lost their television shows. The pervasive, expressly Christian atmosphere suits most of these performers who regularly give stage testimonials, especially at Christmastime. The great majority in the audiences appreciates this point of view; "Amen" and "Praise the Lord" are sometimes heard during a performance. The audiences are primarily fans from the old days, and their shows are consequently devoted to their "greatest hits"; if you didn't know them in their heyday, you may not enjoy them as much.

Many shows reach back even further. The people most likely to take bus tours or lengthy vacations are older, often retired citizens with leisure time; the performers are obviously going to play up the music these audiences loved when they were younger—music from the late 30s and 40s as well as the 50s and 60s. Older audiences may also seem less demonstrative and more conservative than the ones you may be used to in other theatrical centers. And since the Branson/Lakes area has become a popular retirement center, a greater and greater percentage of the resident population is older. (The number of folks are retiring "early" is on the rise, so a growing number of the tourist guides, volunteers, and in some cases, the semi-amateur entertainers you will encounter are older.)

Branson is, finally, a problematic destination for anyone confined to a wheelchair or even heavily dependent on a cane or walker. It is, after all, in the Ozarks, and many of the parking lots are extremely steep. The older theaters especially are erratically accessible, and not all of the restrooms, even in newer or renovated venues, are fully outfitted. If you or a member of your group uses a wheelchair, we suggest you make advance inquiries about the facilities at each place you plan to visit; although we have included some of that information in the individual descriptions later in the book, situations may change or your requirements may be even more specific.

If it seems odd that we would include these caveats, it's probably because you're not familiar with our guides. We are not just travel boosters, and not everything we say in this book will be favorable. But it will be what we actually believe and what we've experienced. We at the *Unofficial Guide* series are dedicated to making your vacations and business trips as pleasant as possible, and we don't want you to visit someplace that won't suit you.

So Why Branson?

We prepared this guide because we think there are many good reasons to visit Branson—even for those not overly fond of "old-fashioned" country humor or gospel music. All things considered, it's an entertainment bargain. Ticket prices and hotel rooms are reasonable, especially compared to other vacation destinations, and the restaurants are certainly cheaper, even the fancier ones. Plus, there are fewer incidental costs. For example, unlike in Las Vegas, there are no maître d's to tip to get better seats, since nearly all the theaters, even the smallest, have computerized ticketing. The practice of tipping, in fact, is almost entirely limited to restaurants, bar staff, and hotel maids. (There are a whole lot of ways to save even more money, as we'll discuss in the next chapter.) There's also a health bonus: no smoking is allowed inside any theater in town. The folks in Branson want you to come back again next year.

The local Bransonites are extremely friendly and hospitable in a way you may nearly have forgotten. The performers themselves are personally accessible, photo- and autograph-friendly to a degree unknown in New York or Las Vegas. In terms of variety, there is some fine swing, big band, and Western traditional music, quite a bit of 50s doo-wop and early rock and roll, and a good smattering of bluegrass. The Grand Palace in particular has brought in a number of more contemporary stars—Dwight Yoakam, Vince Gill, Reba McEntire, Lorrie Morgan, and Neal McCoy, even Bill Cosby—for limited engagements.

So just do a little advance work: read our tips, our theater and production profiles, and our hotel and restaurant ratings before planning your visit. In particular, we suggest you look over the sections entitled "Before You Go" and "Getting Around, Getting Along." We think you'll find a lot to your liking.

A Little History of the Area

American history buffs might remember a few things about the Ozark region. It was, after all, the "Missouri Compromise" of 1820 that brought in Missouri as a slave state, foreshadowing the eventual division of the country. Like its neighboring states, Missouri was sundered by rival slavery and abolition forces: "Free State" Kansans and pro-slavery Missourians knocked heads not only across the border but within families.

After the war, Missouri was further splintered by dispossessed or war-disoriented marauders and outlaws, including Frank and Jesse James (who never made it quite as far south as Branson), and the Bald Knobbers, the local vigilantes who got their name by lighting signal fires from the bald knobs (cleared tops) of hills. They appear in their original violent guise in the outdoor theater production of *The Shepherd of the Hills* (see the chapter "Theme Parks, Museums, and Other Attractions"), but were recast as comic mascots when local history became entertainment.

Situated in one of the finest outdoor recreation areas in the Ozarks, Branson was a fishing and summer haven more than a century ago. In 1913, the construction of Ozark Beach Dam turned a section of the river into Lake Taneycomo (a contraction of "Taney County, Mo.") and also created Bull Shoals Lake to the south. In the 1950s, a second dam, Table Rock, 22 miles upriver, formed Table Rock Lake, which is now the camping and water-sports center, and transformed Lake Taneycomo into a cold-water compound stocked with trout from a nearby farm. A lot of the veteran fishermen don't even come into "town" anymore, preferring to bypass the traffic and head straight for the water.

THE BRANSON MUSIC SCENE

The Branson music saga is said to date from 1960, when the Herschend family opened an old-timey Ozarks village park with a steam train and music at Marvel Cave on West Highway 76. Now known as Silver Dollar City, the park has grown through the years into a major entertainment enterprise. In the Branson area, in partnership with Kenny Rogers, it also owns the Grand Palace theater, the Showboat *Branson Belle,* and the Dixie Stampede. Outside of Missouri, Silver Dollar owns the Dollywood park in Pigeon Forge, Tennessee, as well as two other Dixie Stampedes.

The area is also the setting for the country's first million-selling novel, Harold Bell Wright's *The Shepherd of the Hills,* published in 1907. Around 1960, about the same time that Silver Dollar City opened, the owners of the farm on which Bell based his book launched an outdoor pageant version of *The Shepherd of the Hills* that is still performed today. Not long after, the five Mabe brothers introduced their old-fashioned country variety show, called the *Baldknobbers Jamboree,* first performing down near Lake Taneycomo and then moving into Branson on Highway 76 ("the Strip"). In 1967, a year before the Mabe family moved into town, the Presley family moved their *Presleys' Country Jubilee* onto the Strip from Talking Rocks Cavern where they had performed since 1963.

Growth in Branson was slow until 1983, when Roy Clark became the first national celebrity performer to establish a permanent venue. (Being one of the first probably explains how he got that Country Boulevard lucky phone number—"0076.") Tourism picked up at an increasing rate through the 80s; and by 1990, Mel Tillis, Shoji Tabuchi, Christy Lane, Mickey

Gilley, Jim Stafford, and Moe Bandy were all installed. Andy Williams followed in 1991, and the floodgates opened.

Middle American Music

Branson entertainment, not surprisingly, reflects the immense hold that radio (and later, television) have held over the South and Midwest. One of Branson's repertory groups, the Ozark Jubilee, has its roots in the Red Foley TV show of the 1950s. In the same way, Branson reflects a very specific generation gap: the "radio" is primarily 1930s to mid-1960s and the television is pre-MTV. The old-timey, almost vaudeville entertainment that the Grand Ole Opry and other Southern and Midwestern radio jamborees used to broadcast weekly is vigorously maintained here by the Presleys and Baldknobbers. The TV variety-show sophistication of Andy Williams and Glen Campbell, not to mention the living-room dance floor sweep of *The Lawrence Welk Show,* are recreated almost exactly. Gospel music, which still dominates Sunday radio throughout the South and Midwest, has a very strong presence in Branson as well.

It's all family-oriented, which is one major reason there is so little "modern" or urban-style music. No lyric in any show can offend or confuse anyone. There may be some outhouse humor, particularly in the old-time shows, but no X-rated language or behavior is tolerated. A Chippendale's-style male strip show closed down.

Branson has one other claim to fame: Ozark artist Rosie O'Neill, who invented the Kewpie doll. Her home, Bonniebrook, is the site of an annual Kewpiesta festival in April, and a life-size, albeit somewhat battered, version of a Kewpie.

About This Guide

How Come "Unofficial"?

While other guidebooks have been written about Branson, few have been evaluative. Most "official" guides to Branson tout the big stars, promote the local restaurants and hotels indiscriminately, and leave out a lot of good stuff. Some guides come close to regurgitating the hotels' and tourist offices' own promotional material.

This one is different. Instead of pandering to the tourist industry, we'll tell you if it's not worth the wait for the mediocre food served in a well-known restaurant, we'll complain loudly about shows (and under-padded seats), and we'll guide you away from the crowds and lines for a break now and then. If a museum is boring or a three-hour melodrama is a ham festival, we say so—and, in the process, we hope to make your visit more fun, efficient, and economical.

In preparing this book, nothing was taken for granted. Virtually every theater, amusement or theme park, hotel, restaurant, shop, and attraction was visited by a team of trained observers who conducted detailed evaluations and rated each according to formal criteria. Team members talked with tourists of all ages to determine what they enjoyed most *and least* during their Branson visit.

Although our observers are independent and impartial, they do not claim to have special expertise. Like you, they visited Branson as tourists, noting their satisfaction or dissatisfaction. The primary difference between the average tourist and the trained evaluator is the evaluator's skills in organization, preparation, and observation. The trained evaluator is responsible for much more than simply observing and cataloging. While the average tourist is gazing in awe at the laser light display at Shoji Tabuchi Theatre, for instance, the professional is rating the show in terms of pace, the location of rest rooms, how quickly lines move, and whether children will find the show entertaining. The evaluator also checks out things such as other nearby attractions, alternative places to go if the line at a main attraction is too long, and where to find the best local lunch options. Observer teams use detailed checklists to analyze hotel rooms, restaurants, and attractions. Finally, evaluator ratings and observations are integrated with tourist reactions and the opinions of patrons for a comprehensive quality profile of each feature and service.

In compiling this guide, we recognize that tourists' ages, backgrounds, and interests will strongly influence their taste in Branson's wide array of activities and attractions and will account for a preference for one show or theater over another. Our sole objective is to provide the reader with sufficient description, critical evaluation, and pertinent data to make knowledgeable decisions according to individual tastes.

Branson is a city built on show business, and we dared them to show us the works. We sent in a team of evaluators who toured each site, ate in the city's restaurants, performed critical evaluations of its hotels, and visited almost every theater, rental hall, and variety venue in town.

A DIFFERENT KIND OF GUIDEBOOK

We got into the guidebook business because we were unhappy with the way travel guides make the reader work to get any usable information. Most guidebooks are compilations of lists. This is true regardless of whether the information is presented in list form or artfully distributed through pages of prose. There is insufficient detail in a list, and prose presentation can be tedious and contain large helpings of nonessential or marginally useful information. Not enough wheat for nourishment in one instance, too much chaff in the other. Either way, these guides provide little more than departure points from which readers initiate their own quests.

Even readable and well-researched guides can give you so much undifferentiated information that readers generally have no alternative but to work through all the write-ups before beginning to narrow their choices. Recommendations, if any, lack depth and conviction. Such guides compound problems rather than solve them, by failing to narrow travelers' choices down to a thoughtfully considered, well-distilled, and manageable few.

Travelers want quick answers as opposed to endless alternatives, and they care about the author's opinion. (The author, after all, is supposed to know what he is talking about.) Therefore, a guidebook should be explicit, prescriptive, and, above all, direct. The *Unofficial Guide* tries to do just that. It spells out alternatives and recommends specific courses of action. It simplifies complicated destinations and attractions and allows the traveler to feel in control in the most unfamiliar environment. The objective of the *Unofficial Guide* is not to have all the information or even the most information, but to have the most accessible, useful information, unbiased by affiliation with any organization or industry.

The *Unofficial Guide to Branson, Missouri* is designed for individuals and families traveling for the fun of it, especially those visiting Branson for the first time. The guide is directed at value-conscious, consumer-oriented adults who seek a cost-effective, yet comfortable travel style.

SPECIAL FEATURES

The *Unofficial Guide* offers the following special features:

- Frank recommendations for—and against—celebrity shows and tourist attractions.
- Ideas for "clustering" attractions, cutting down on travel time, and staying near the attraction you most want to visit.
- "Best bargain" hints and insider "tips" to help you get the most value and fun from each attraction.
- Ways to design a trip that best suits you, your kids, and/or your parents.
- How to "cram" the most entertainment into your trip.
- Listings keyed to your interests, so you can pick and choose.

- Advice to sight-seers on how to avoid the worst of the crowds, circumvent traffic, and slash excessive costs.

- Shortcuts and maps to make it easy to find places you want to go to and avoid places you don't.

- Insider advice on crowds, clothes, comfort, and convenience; tips on making your neighbor's visit more pleasurable, too.

- A detailed index and table of contents to help you find things fast.

What you won't get:

- Long, useless lists where everything looks the same.

- Information that gets you somewhere you want to go at the worst possible time.

- Information without advice on how to use it.

LETTERS, COMMENTS, AND QUESTIONS FROM READERS

We expect to learn from our mistakes as well as from the input of our readers, and to improve with each book and edition. Many of those who use the *Unofficial Guides* write to us asking questions, making comments, or sharing their own discoveries and lessons learned on trips to cities we've written about. We appreciate all input, both positive and critical, and encourage our readers to continue writing. Readers' comments and observations frequently are incorporated in revised editions of the *Unofficial Guide.*

How to Write the Authors

Eve Zibart and Bob Sehlinger
The Unofficial Guide to Branson, Missouri
Box 43673
Birmingham, AL 35243

When you write, be sure to put your return address on your letter as well as on the envelope—sometimes envelopes and letters get separated. And remember, our work takes us out of the office for long periods of time, so forgive us if our response is delayed.

Reader Survey

At the back of the guide you will find a short questionnaire that you can use to express opinions concerning your Branson visit. Clip the questionnaire along the dotted line and mail it to the above address.

Part One

Planning Your Visit to Branson

Gathering Information

The first thing you should do—ideally, several weeks or months before you actually plan to visit Branson—is contact the Branson/Lakes Chamber of Commerce, P.O. Box 1897, Branson, MO 65615-1897; (417) 334-4136. The Chamber has an astonishing stockpile of information brochures, and the staff are unusually friendly and helpful. The brochures list up-to-date attractions, and many of them have discount offers and coupons to clip out. The Chamber also has phone numbers and flyers for local tour and ticket packagers (see the following section) and listings for hotels, camp-grounds, and so forth.

You may not see the most useful publications until you actually get into town or into your hotel room. We particularly recommend the "Ozark Mountain Visitor," published bimonthly by the *Branson News.* It offers information on new shows, restaurants, shopping options, and, of course, coupons. Although the "Ozark Mountain Visitor" is free *in* Branson, you may want to order in advance or even subscribe if you visit Branson more than once a year or plan to stay longer than a week. Call (417) 334-3161 ($7 a copy, $25 a year).

The big tour and ticket packagers can also supply you with lists of shows and accommodations; a good way to find those businesses is to flip through the travel sections of the Sunday paper or the backs of travel magazines. If your local paper doesn't list anything helpful, go to a newsstand and get a paper from someplace closer like St. Louis or Kansas City. Or call a travel agent and ask about packages for Branson.

Two internet destinations have information about Branson. At www.bestreadguide.com you can make hotel reservations, learn about events and attractions, restaurants, and so on. At http://bransonnews.com you can read about Branson's news, stars, "and more."

When to Go

AVOIDING THE CROWDS

Generally speaking, the fall color season and the early summer up through the Fourth of July are the busiest times of year, followed by spring. There is a lot of activity surrounding the Thanksgiving and Christmas holidays, but otherwise November and December are slow. January and February are the least busy times of all.

If you have small children, you may have to work around school schedules, but that's not as much of a problem as you might think, because in Branson the late summer, especially the last few weeks of August, is actually a "slack" season. In fact, you have to be careful, because sometimes business drops off so much right before the Labor Day boom that theaters may cancel their afternoon shows. Some even shut down altogether; ask about refunds in such cases.

Simply put, weekends are more crowded than weekdays year-round. Most of Branson's theaters are situated along Highway 76, a mostly two-lane road that can rival any Los Angeles freeway when it comes to traffic congestion. On weekends, particularly between 4 p.m. and 10 p.m., you can age considerably trying to drive from one end of the Strip to the other. Our advice is to avoid weekends if possible.

OTHER CONSIDERATIONS

Unless you are going on business, you might want to pick the dates for your visit by first deciding what you want to see or do. For example, there are special events throughout the year, from the Pro-Celebrity Fish-Off and Kewpiesta in April to the popular Ozark Mountain Christmas season and informal "Festival of Lights" decorating competition in November and December (the Nativity scene across Mount Branson features 40-foot-tall lighted figures). Check the Special Events calendar below.

If you're going for the fishing, you can pretty much pick any season, but the best months include October (for brown trout), March (for bass, including the largemouth), April (catfish and crappie), and even late winter (rainbow trout). Note that trout anglers must have a Missouri Trout Stamp in addition to a fishing license at Lake Taneycomo. Most area liquor stores are empowered to provide hunting and fishing licenses. (See the chapter, "The Great Outdoors" for more information.)

April is famous for dogwood blossoms and redbuds, particularly along the Ozark Country Dogwood Trail in Forsyth, Missouri, to the east on Highway 76, and in nearby Kimberling City, just west of Table Rock Lake on Highway 13. If you're a hiker or biker, the autumn color is spectacular in the wooded hills (see "The Great Outdoors" again), and there are lots of arts and crafts and food festivals as well.

January and February are off-season; in fact, all theaters used to close between Christmas and April. However, an increasing number of shows are advertising year-round performances, and Branson weather is fairly mild. Statistically, temperatures rarely go below the 20s, even in January. The catch here is that the roads, being hilly and difficult for some people to negotiate even in good weather, can be dangerous in a winter storm. Also, shows might be canceled during bad winter weather. If you decide to go during the winter, just make sure you inquire about refunds or reticketing policies and bring a couple of good books.

Branson Weather

Generally, winter temperatures stay in the 40s during the day and 20s at night; beginning in April, daytime highs range from 63° to 72°, with lows in the 40s. From June through August and well into September, highs stay in the 80s and lows in the high 50s or 60s. Even November averages highs in the 50s and lower 60s.

Precipitation is fairly light in all seasons. If you want to carry an umbrella, fine—but for the sake of your fellow theatergoers, get the collapsible type. Otherwise, it won't be just the dancers who are tripping down the aisles.

What to Pack

In terms of wardrobe, the keynote is casual. You should read the sections, "What to Wear Around Town" and "What to Wear (The Inside Story)" in the chapter, "The Etiquette of Branson" before planning your packing, particularly when it comes to shoes. The only major variable, of course, is your coat or other wrap; even then you should remember that you'll be constantly putting it on and taking it off. You may have a terrific down jacket guaranteed to block sub-zero winds, but if it has 14 toggle ties and triple zippers, you'll be exhausted after the first day. And because you'll also have to hold your coat on your lap or sit on it in the theater, you might have an easier time with a shorter-length coat or jacket.

Fur, incidentally, is a fairly new issue in Branson. The big stars probably wear it, and there is no particular animal rights group in town that might object, but only a very few theaters have a coat check room, and fur can be cumbersome to clutch. We'd say that in this case, you should settle for lining or trim rather than your best Blackglama.

Special Events Calendar

These are some of the annual events held in and around Branson. For specific dates and updated information, contact the Chamber of Commerce at (417) 334-4136. Or for information on particular festivals at the theme parks, etc., contact the parks directly (see park profiles later in the book).

JANUARY

This is "down season" as far as most of the theaters are concerned, though some are now open year-round (see individual descriptions).

FEBRUARY

Many theaters are still closed. Vulture Venture, held at the Shepherd of the Hills Fish Hatchery, features storytelling, live vulture programs, and kid's activities, usually occurs the first Saturday in February. (417) 334-4865.

MARCH

Branson World Fest, held mid-month at a major theater, officially kicks off the spring season with a combination meet-the-stars, taste of the town, and preview of the shows. (417) 334-4136. The World's Fishing Fair is held at the end of the month at Springfield's Bass Pro Shops, and includes a casting competition and visits with nationally known anglers. (417) 873-5111. The IPRA-sanctioned Cowboy Classic Rodeo is held at the Ozark Empire Fairgrounds the last week in March. (417) 833-2660.

APRIL

Branson World Fest, held at Silver Dollar City, usually begins the second week of April and runs through the second week of May. More than 250 performers from around the world bring their music, culture, and dance to Branson. (800) 952-6626. Bonniebrook, the home of Kewpie creator Rosie O'Neill, holds its annual doll festival, the Kewpiesta, in mid-April. (417) 561-2250. (417) 833-2660. Springfield's Frisco Days Festival, held in mid-April, celebrates the coming of the Iron Horse. (417) 864-7015. Springfield's Ozarks Kennel Club Dog Show is held in late-April. (417) 833-2660.

MAY

Plumb Nellie Days, Hillbilly Festival and Craft Show, is held in mid-May in Branson. The show features crafters from around the Midwest as well as entertainment and children's activities. (800) 214-3661. Springfield hosts the NSRA Mid-America Street Rod National Car Show in mid-May. (417) 833-2660. Branson Remembers . . . A Memorial Tribute is held over Memorial Day weekend. Over thirty special events and services are held. (417) 337-8387. Springfield's Arts Fest is held the first weekend in May. (417) 869-8380. The Great American Music Festival begins in mid-May and runs through the first week in June at Silver Dollar City. Two hundred musicians perform on stages throughout the theme park. (800) 952-6626.

JUNE

Silver Dollar City hosts the National Children's Festival from Mid-June to mid-August. The festival features nationally known children's performers. (800) 952-6626. The Springfield Walking Horse Show is held in late June at Ozark Empire Fairgrounds. (417) 833-2660. Springfield Art Museum's Watercolor USA competition draws contestants from across the country in June. (417) 837-5700. Springfield's Frisco Days Festival, held in early June, celebrates the coming of the Iron Horse. (417) 864-7015.

JULY

Branson's Spirit of '76 Independence Day Celebration runs for four days, and includes fishing, food, fireworks, watersports, and music. (417) 337-8387. The Ozark Empire fair is held in Springfield beginning in late July. (417) 833-2660.

AUGUST

Branson's Annual Oldtime Fiddle Contest is held in mid-August. Fiddlers from all over the country gather at the Taneycomo lakefront to compete. (417) 334-1548. The Nike Ozark Open golf tournament is held in Springfield in August. (417) 887-3400. The Fall Hunting Classic is held at Bass Pro Shops in Springfield in late August. The show includes the World Championship 3-D Archery Tournament, as well as appearances by nationally known professional hunters. (417) 873-5111. Springfield holds the Ozark Antique Auto Swap Meet, with over 1,000 booths in late August. (417) 833-2660.

SEPTEMBER

Silver Dollar City hosts the National Festival of Craftsmen, featuring 150 artists, for two months beginning in early September, (800) 952-6626. The Branson Annual Free Fall Harvest runs from mid-September to mid-October, and features two and a half tons of pumpkins and over 15 different arts and crafts booths. (417) 334-4191. Autumn Daze Craft Festival and Sidewalk sale is held in Branson mid-September. (417) 334-1548. The Midwest Walking Horse Show is held at Ozark Empire Fairgrounds in late September. (417) 833-2660. Springfield hosts the Ozark Piecemakers Quilt Show in late September. (417) 581-6831.

OCTOBER

Springfield's Halloween Spooktacular features hundreds of hand carved pumpkins. (417) 864-1800. The bi-annual Ozarks Kennel Club Dog Show occurs in mid-October. (417) 833-2660. A Fall Rodeo is held at Ozark Empire Fairgrounds in late October. (417) 833-2660.

NOVEMBER

Branson hosts the Veteran's Homecoming, which includes patriotic salutes to veterans, the week leading up to Veteran's Day. (417) 337-8387. On Veteran's day, Branson holds an annual Parade and Ceremony. The parade begins at the Railway station, winds through downtown, and ends with a ceremony at the Taneycomo lakefront. (417) 334-4136. Branson's Old Time Christmas lasts for the duration of November and December at Silver Dollar City. Special events include Christmas choirs, a five story Christmas tree, and a talking Christmas tree. (800) 952-6626. Shepherd of the Hills presents the Holiday Homestead and Trail of Lights and Holiday Homestead. After dusk, lights, motion, and music are featured on the drive-through Trail of Lights. During the day, a special "Remember When" show is performed. (417) 334-4191.

DECEMBER

The Candlelight Christmas Open House is held in early December in downtown Branson. (417) 334-1548. Branson's Annual Adoration Christmas Parade and Lighting is held in early December. This nocturnal parade is held downtown and includes over 70 marching units and floats. (417) 334-4136. On New Year's Eve, Springfield hosts First Night, a celebration of the performing arts. (417) 869-8380.

Getting Tickets to the Shows

Assuming you want to see at least some of the theatrical performances while you're in town, and assuming you want to see some particular shows, you have another decision to make: How involved do you want to get in planning your trip? We suggest you read this section before deciding what role to take, because it could save you quite a bit of money.

If you buy a package or take a chartered tour, of course, you pretty much have to go where the bus is going. If you don't mind that, or are with a group of friends, there are advantages—not just the package rates, but the special seating and access most theaters provide for tour buses. Entertainers here pay a lot of attention to the bread-and-butter stuff, and buttering up tour groups is high on that list. Birthdays and anniversaries get saluted from the stage, theaters with difficult parking lots usually have special parking lanes and even entranceways for tour buses (which can be a huge plus if members of your party are disabled or elderly), and tour groups often get the best seats, within easy photo-distance of the stars.

On the other hand, if you are not going during the busiest times, and don't care which shows you attend, you may prefer to see the lay of the land for yourself. Order the big-show tickets you want in advance, then scout around for matinees, limited engagements, or novelty shows that interest you. During the holiday seasons in particular, you may find some big name acts not usually part of the Branson repetoire.

Ticket and Reservation Services

There are dozens of tour groups, travel packagers, and ticket buyers who will take care of buying tickets for you; the promotional material available from the Chamber of Commerce lists many of them. Depending on how specific your wants and needs are, you can turn over the whole vacation, the entertainment, the lodging, or just particular tickets to a pro.

There are drawbacks to using a middleman. Some ticket vendors allow you to choose only within a certain "show group," meaning that you can only choose one ticket from list A, two from list B, and one from list C—sort of like the old Chinese menu joke. Others, usually the ticket services themselves, will get precisely the shows you order, although there may be a surcharge. Ozark Ticket and Travel, (417) 336-3432, offers a choice: They will not only get your seats, but will pick up the tickets and deliver them to your motel, or simply reserve the seats and get you a voucher to take to the theater. The first service costs $2.95 per ticket, the second option $2.50 per ticket; so even for just two people, that can add as much as $10 a day to your visit. However, you may well consider the convenience worth the money.

Other ticket reservation services include Branson Hotline, (800) 523-7589; Branson Ticket Centers, (888) 277-4697; All Branson Tickets, (800) 678-7876; and That's the Ticket, (800) 860-5127.

Self-Service in Branson

Getting your own tickets is not hugely taxing, and you should consider making at least some of your own arrangements. Often you can get good tickets just by walking up to the box offices (a few days or at least hours in advance is safest). Most theaters have the seating chart on a computer screen, and can show you just what's available. Even after you enter the theater, if the show is not sold out, and you ask the usher nicely, you may be able to move to another unoccupied seat. (Politeness is essential here, so if you're accustomed to going *attitude à attitude* with hoity-toity maître d's, get a new style fast.) If a show is sold out, many theaters release uncollected reservations an hour before showtime, so you might try coming back anyway. If you're in town for more than a couple of days, you may be able to upgrade by exchanging for tickets on a different night: most theaters require 48-hour advance notice for exchanges.

Self-Service Before Leaving Home

You can reserve tickets before leaving home by contacting the individual theater box offices. If you want to make sure you sit in exactly the right spot and so on, you can negotiate your order specifics over the phone. It can be cheaper (depending on whether the box offices you want to call have toll-free numbers or not) and more informative (the operators in Branson are apt to give you a tip or tell you about a special promotion). Phone numbers for all theaters are included in the individual descriptions in the book, along with basic ticket prices at press time; these may change slightly, but ticket inflation has been fairly slight so far.

Most theaters accept major credit cards for orders without adding a service fee. Some theaters may charge a couple of dollars if you want tickets mailed—you probably should not have them mailed unless you have ordered at least three weeks in advance—but you can just pick them up at the box office in advance of the show.

However, in many cases you can, if you call yourself, get reservations without putting out any up-front money. If you want to see Kenny Rogers at the Grand Palace, for example, you can call toll-free and make reservations, consulting with their bank of well-trained and helpful operators on where you want to sit and how much you want to spend. At that point, you have the choice of actually buying the tickets using a credit card, which ensures you'll get into the show even if you arrive late, or simply making the reservations and picking up the tickets at the box office, preferably several hours or a day before the show.

This is a particularly good bet for travelers whose schedule (or health, or tangible assets) may be a little uncertain; you won't be out any money.

It might also guard against unexpected changes of schedule or performer at the theater itself. Most theaters warn that artists are subject to change without notice, right above the line that reads, "Non-transferable. No refunds." Of course, the only time the ticket clerks are apt to check your ID is when you pick up orders paid in advance, so in theory you could swap or sell them off to somebody else—but if you don't want to see the substitute performer, nobody else you know may either.

Besides, if you happen to be walking around town getting oriented and someone hands you one of those $2 discount coupons marked "Present at time of ticket purchase," you may get an even better deal. The drawback is that, as the theaters note, schedules and prices are subject to change without notice. Conceivably you may find the ticket is more expensive later, but as we said, the price creep so far has been extremely slight.

As mentioned, reserved tickets *not* picked up at the box office by one hour before curtain time are released and put back into the pool for sale. This suggests two other tips: if a show is supposedly sold out on the night you want to go, you can take a chance on arriving at 7:10 and asking if any seats have been released. Or you can ask to have your tickets upgraded if you couldn't get the seats you wanted.

If you are on your own, it is important to understand that huge blocks of seats, particularly for the most popular shows, are reserved months in advance by tour operators and packagers. If you cannot get the seat you want for the performance that best suits your schedule, ask the theater box office for the names and phone numbers of any wholesalers, packagers, or tour operators who are holding blocks of tickets. If the box office will not release this information to you, have your travel agent call. Having obtained the names and numbers, call the block holders and try to buy a ticket. If they have not sold out their tour or package, they will be glad to sell their unused tickets to you or your travel agent. If ticket block holders do not sell all of their ticket inventory by a certain date, usually three to seven weeks before the date of the show, unsold tickets will be returned to the theater.

The Other Big Ticket Question: How Much?

As we said, Branson is a relative bargain, especially if you're used to paying for show tickets in New York, Los Angeles, or Chicago. At press time, adult tickets range from about $12 to $40.

The only rule is: Don't Pay Full Price If You Can Help It. Branson businesses may be in friendly competition, but it's still competition, and you should take advantage of it. As one Branson theater manager put it, "Never pay full price until you check the coupons: 'Sleep here for free!'

'Eat here free!' 'Kids free!' 'Second show free!' If you're young and have kids, if you're old and have Social Security, if you just keep asking, you can always cut the bill."

Many theaters have a range of "special fares," such as AAA or AARP or senior citizen discounts, and nearly any group of 20 or more gets a deal, too. The bigger venues may have different prices for seats in different areas, and if you're younger or don't need to be close up to see or hear well, you can do fine farther back or up in the balcony. In fact, in a few cases, the upstairs or side aisle views are better; see our critiques of the individual venues.

Many theaters have half-price or even free tickets for children under 12. When times are slow, especially in August, a lot of performers beef up their special promotions to try to lure in the dwindling business. Handouts advertising shows often include discount coupons on single tickets or even a whole party.

If the same company owns more than one attraction, it probably has a package rate: for example, Silver Dollar City also owns the showboat *Branson Belle,* Dixie Stampede, and White Water, and frequently offers combination tickets including two or more attractions. Savings vary from 5 to 20% off of regular ticket prices, depending on how many attractions you include in you package. Call (800) 5-PALACE. And they don't have to be used on the same day, meaning you can take advantage of the park's own two-hour evening show and spread your investment over two days.

Even shows that aren't directly connected to a restaurant or other attraction often have small discount offers. Always check your ticket stubs, too; some offer one or two dollars off a souvenir or concession.

The amusement parks also have extended-use passes that will save repeat visitors money: a regular one-day ticket for Silver Dollar City, for example, costs an adult $33 and a child $23, and season passes, good for the calendar year, are $55 and $45.

Even if you don't do any of this in advance, you can cut a few dollars here and there. Nearly every brochure, newsletter, and tourist magazine has some special coupons inside, offering everything from show ticket and amusement park discounts (usually one or two dollars but sometimes more), to free souvenir rainbow mugs at Waltzing Waters, to a two-for-one deal at 76 Music Hall, to a pair of dinner-show tickets on the *Polynesian Princess* river cruise, and even half-price second entrees at restaurants. These brochures are available not only at the Chamber of Commerce and tourist information stations, but in many hotel lobbies, hotel rooms, and shopping malls.

Part Two

Lodging and Camping

Branson Lodging

SEASONS

Demand for accommodations in Branson is very predictable. Summer and the October fall color season are the busiest, most crowded times of year. Christmas, Easter, Thanksgiving, and other major holiday periods are also brisk. January and February are pretty dead, so certain shows will be closed and even some highways are occasionally closed due to snow or ice. The best months for small crowds, good weather, and bargain accommodations are September, mid-November, the first two weeks of December, late March, April, and May. Branson and the Ozarks are very popular for weekend getaways, so regardless of the time of year, weekends are busier than weekdays.

When visiting the mountains, most visitors either drive their own cars or book a motorcoach tour. For those who enjoy group travel, motorcoach tours often offer both value and convenience. The downside of group touring, always, is the regimentation. If you are considering a motorcoach tour, first make sure the tour itinerary is consistent with your vacation agenda. Second, check the hotel the tour uses against the hotel ratings in this chapter. A tour packager's choice of hotels speaks volumes about the overall quality of the tour.

Alternative lodging, in the form of tent camping, RV camping, country inns, bed-and-breakfasts, and even houseboat rentals, is readily available in the Branson area and is discussed below.

GATHERING INFORMATION

In addition to this guide, you may wish to obtain some of the free information available from the Branson Chamber of Commerce, (417) 334-4136, which will send you a whole packet of information on hotels, campgrounds, shows, marinas, restaurants, attractions, and recreational opportunities in the area.

HOTEL AND MOTEL OVERVIEW

Because Branson's current incarnation as a showtown is a recent phenomenon, most of its hotels and motels are pretty new. In fact, there has been a veritable lodging boom in and near Branson during the 1990s. At the end of 1997, there were 23,000 guest rooms within a ten-mile radius, more than twice as many as had existed only six years earlier. Growth is a little bit out of control in Branson, and nobody is quite sure how (or if) the hotel supply and demand equation will balance. For the present, however, visitors can enjoy new rooms at very reasonable rates.

For the most part, Branson lodging is homogeneous: you could fall asleep in one hotel room, be moved to another during the night, and on awakening never know the difference. There are miles of side-by-side Holiday Inn and Motel 6 clones where the operative word is cleanliness, not style. At Disneyland, attendants admonish tourists to write down the section, row, and space where they park. "This is a big lot, and all these parking spaces look pretty much the same. You don't want to be looking around for your car after a long day at the park." The same goes for lodging in Branson: better jot down the name of your motel.

Most Branson hotel rooms look alike inside, and what you see when you peek out the window won't be all that different either. Very few Branson hotel rooms offer a pleasant view. This is surprising and disappointing to us, given that Branson is promoted as an Ozark Mountain resort town. Clearly, in Branson, the mountain setting is all but incidental. There are, of course, exceptions to this epidemic of homogeneity. Two examples are the Big Cedar Lodge in nearby Ridgedale, Missouri, and the Branson Lodge, an older motel on Highway 165.

The Big Cedar Lodge is by far the most beautiful resort in the Ozarks, offering lodge rooms, cabins, conference facilities, and the area's best restaurant. Everything, from the open beam ceilings of the main lodge to the spectacular view of the valley below, is imaginatively conceived and masterfully executed. Originally built as a sportsman's retreat, the Big Cedar Lodge resembles in many ways the extraordinary national park lodges of the 1920s.

The Branson Lodge by contrast is a modest property, a small motel built long before Branson became a showtown. What distinguishes the Branson Lodge is that every guest room is decorated in a different antique motif and that all of the furnishings are for sale! If the bed you sleep in is especially comfortable, you can (for a price) take it home with you.

By far, the best room for the money in Branson is at the Bradford Inn. Each room has a unique decor that is continuously updated. If you'd enjoy a private deck with a wonderful view or a jacuzzi (or both!), be sure to ask—the additional charge is much less than you might imagine.

A Word about Branson Resorts

In the Branson area, lodging properties situated on rivers or lakes tend to refer to themselves (almost without exception) as "resorts." Few of these places, however, offer the amenities normally associated with a bona fide resort, i.e., restaurant, lounge, golf course, spa, clubhouse, concierge, bell services, etc. Most, in fact, are more like fishing camps, featuring small cabins with minimal furnishings, a lake or river front, a boat ramp, a modest pool, and sometimes a dock or boathouse. While many of these properties are quite charming and scenic, resorts they are not.

Cabins and Condominiums

Most Branson motels and hotels offer not-so-beautiful views of highways, parking lots, and goofy golf courses. While, of course, there are exceptions, we nevertheless recommend renting a cabin or condo as the best way to enjoy the mountains. Some private cabins and condos can be had for about the price of a motel room, and include such amenities as full kitchens, decks, fireplaces, and even hot tubs. Most important, in our estimation, however, is that the cabins and condos provide exactly the kind of quiet, solitude, and remote beauty that most folks come to the mountains to experience.

Where cabins are free-standing structures, condominiums are usually part of a large development and almost always share a common wall with adjoining units on either side. Many condos, however, offer the same features as cabins. While cabins do not usually offer swimming pools or golf courses, condominium complexes frequently do.

It should be mentioned that "cabin" in the Ozarks covers a bewildering range of structures. Generally when you see the word "cabin" in relation to an Ozark Mountain "resort," you are talking about a small, spartan affair more reminiscent of a YMCA camp than of a private home or luxury condo. Some are log, but most are plywood, A-framed buildings with one or two small bedrooms and a combination living/dining area.

These cabins, ubiquitous in the Branson area, are generally rated in the Motel 6/budget category by our *Unofficial Guide* hotel inspectors, and are not really what we are recommending here. Nicer cabins or private homes are available for rent, but are much more rare in the Ozarks than in the Smokies or Rockies. The Woods, (800) 935-2345, rents upscale cabins on a regular basis. For private home rentals and properties available on an irregular basis contact Pointe Royale Realtors at (800) 627-0160.

While the selection of nice cabins in the Branson area is limited, condos are springing up all over. Most condos offer nightly or weekly rentals. Below is an abbreviated list of condos available for nightly and weekly rentals. For additional listings call the Branson Chamber of Commerce at (417) 334-4136.

Fall Creek Resort	(800) 562-6636
Holiday Hills Golf Course Condos	(800) 225-2422
Lantern Bay Resort Condominiums	(800) 338-0407
Pointe Royale Resort & Golf Course	(800) 962-4710
Rock Lane Resort at Table Rock Lake	(417) 338-2211
Thousand Hills Golf Resort	(800) 693-4653
Treehouse Condos	(800) 328-5199
Village at Indian Point (lake view)	(800) 984-7847

The way to go about renting a cabin or condo is to make a list of features that are important to you. How many beds, bedrooms, and baths do you require? Do you need a full kitchen? When you get your list together, call a rental agency and order your cabin or condo like you would order a pizza. We phoned a Branson agency and said, "We want a two-bedroom, two-bath condo for four adults. We prefer to be high on the mountain, with a good view, in a remote quiet area. We don't care about a hot tub, but we do want a fireplace and a nice big deck." Whether you get what you want depends on how far in advance you make your reservation, the time of year you want to visit, and what you are willing to spend.

When you have figured out what type of accommodation you need, and when you want to go, then you can start shopping. Initiate your search by calling the Branson Chamber of Commerce. Information operators will provide you the names and phone numbers of local agencies and realtors that rent the kind of accommodation you are looking for.

When you talk with a rental agent about a particular cabin or condo, ask how old the property is. If it's older than five or six years, ask if it has been recently renovated. If the property sounds appealing, request that you be mailed photos of both the exterior and interior. Color is better than black and white, but either will do. Some agents have only one set of color photos. If this is the case, suggest that the agent send black and white or color photocopies. Write off any agent that will not supply some sort of photograph. Never reserve a property strictly on the basis of a rendering, sketch, or line drawing. Insist on a photograph.

Be aware that many cabins and condos, while beautiful outside, offer interiors that range from truly tasteless to absolutely bewildering. Country Bordello, Elvis Museum, and Honeymoon Hearts & Ruffles are but three of the major decorating styles alive and well in mountain rental properties. On the other hand, there are many condominiums in Branson which offer very nice guestrooms with disappointing and downright disgusting views. For example, we have seen rooms which include whirlpool bathtubs and full kitchens but do not attempt to conceal the overflowing garbage dumpster or overcrowded trailer park which "graces" the view from the front door.

Once you have found a suitable property, you will usually have to pre-pay two nights with a credit card or check. Some agencies will mail you a rental contract to sign and return, while others will process the whole deal over the phone. Cancellation policies vary, so be sure to inquire.

During the summer, October, and holidays, you will usually have to pay the agency's asking price for your cabin or condo because demand is greater than supply. Other times of year, there is usually room for some negotiation. Some agencies charge a set price for the rental property, while others charge on a per-head basis for the number of persons accommodated. The real savings on cabins and condos occur when two or more couples share a property. Likewise, families that require more than one motel room can also save financially by renting a cabin or condo. Additional savings can be realized by using the kitchen facilities of your rental house rather than going to restaurants.

Particularly during the busier times of year, agencies require a seven-day minimum rental. We were able to work around the minimum, however, by finding properties with two-, three-, or four-day gaps between renters. We found a two-bedroom condo, for example, that was reserved from June 10th through June 16th, and from June 20th to June 26th. The agency was more than happy to rent us the cabin for the short intervening period (June 17, 18, and 19). Reservation gaps, as well as cancellations, are common but unpredictable. You have to call around and ask the right questions to uncover the deals.

The better rentals are reserved well in advance. Some renters sign up for next year during this year's stay. The farther ahead you plan, therefore, the better your chances of getting what you want.

Once the reservation is made, most agents will provide written confirmation. If written confirmation is not routinely provided, ask for it. Along with your confirmation, the agent will also provide directions to the rental office. Most rental offices operate seven days a week during the warm weather months. When you get to the office, you will register, pick up your keys, and be given directions to your rental unit. Once in your cabin or condo, check to make sure that everything is in order. If there is a problem, most agencies offer 24-hour maintenance service.

The majority of area cabins and condos that rent to visitors also work with travel agents. In many cases agents are often able to obtain better prices than can a prospective renter dealing directly with the owner. It's worth a call to your travel agent.

BED-AND-BREAKFASTS AND COUNTRY INNS

Many travelers think of bed-and-breakfasts as a low-cost lodging option. In New York or San Francisco that may be true, but in the Ozarks, B&Bs and country inns frequently offer the most distinctive and luxurious accommodations available. Each guest room is individually and lovingly decorated. Often furnished with antiques, B&B guest rooms offer a refreshing departure from the cloned sameness of Branson hotel rooms. Breakfasts reflect a surprising level of quality and culinary sophistication. Many B&Bs are now able to accommodate dietary restrictions, as well. Not all are so sophisticated, however, so be sure to ask when you book your room.

Most B&Bs and country inns are off the beaten path, and some are situated on lush mountain hillsides or in quiet river valleys. Romantic and peaceful, B&Bs offer a lodging alternative based on personal service and southern hospitality that transcends the sterile, predictable product of chain hotels.

Bed-and-breakfasts are quirky. Most, but not all, B&Bs are open year-round. Some only accept cash or personal checks while others take all major credit cards. Not all rooms come with private baths. Some rooms with private baths may have a tub, but not a shower, or vice versa. Some allow children but not pets; others pets but not children. Many B&Bs provide only the most basic breakfast, while some provide a sumptuous morning feast. Still others offer three meals a day. Most B&Bs are not wheelchair accessible, but it never hurts to ask. Sometimes the host family smokes or has pets, sometimes not.

B&Bs pretty much run the gamut of accommodation styles. You might wind up at someone's home in a room recently vacated when Junior went off to college. Alternatively, you might find yourself in a faux-Victorian establishment designed exclusively to function as a bed-and-breakfast. While country inns are usually larger than B&Bs, the distinction, as well as the level of services offered, is frequently blurred. Because staying at a B&B is like visiting someone in their home, reservations are recommended, though B&Bs or country inns with more than ten rooms usually welcome walk-ins.

To help you sort out your B&B options, we recommend the following guides. Updated regularly, these books describe B&Bs in more detail than is possible in the *Unofficial Guide.*

Recommended Country Inns: The Midwest, by Bob Puhala, published by the Globe Pequot Press. Covers Missouri and eight other midwestern states. To order, phone (800) 243-0495.

Recommended Country Inns: The South, by Sara Pitzer, published by the Globe Pequot Press. Covers Alabama, Kentucky, North Carolina, Florida, Arkansas, Louisiana, South Carolina, Georgia, Mississippi, and Tennessee. To order, phone (800) 243-0495.

Though space limitations preclude describing each of the Branson area B&Bs, we list 15 below that offer nice rooms and a friendly atmosphere. Our favorite area B&Bs are the Bradford Inn on Highway 265 and the Branson House, downtown. The Bradford Inn is new, while the Branson House was established in 1903. Both offer tastefully appointed rooms with private baths. The Branson House has two verandas overlooking the town. The Bradford Inn features decks that provide a spectacular view of the mountains. For these and any of the other B&Bs listed, we suggest you call and request a copy of the B&B's promotional brochure. Some of the B&Bs also are described in the guidebooks referenced above.

Aunt Sadie's Bed and Breakfast	(800) 944-4250
Barger House	(800) 266-2134
Bayside Inn	(417) 337-7478
Bradford Inn	(800) 357-1466
Branson Bed and Breakfast Inn	(417) 335-6104
The Branson House	(417) 334-0959
Brass Swan	(800) 280-6873
Cameron's Crag	(800) 933-8529
Emory Creek B&B	(800) 362-7404
Fall Creek B&B	(800) 482-1090

Free Man House	(800) 583-6101
Grandpa's Farm	(800) 280-5106
Josie's	(800) 289-4125
Schroll's Lakefront	(417) 335-6759
Thurman House	(800) 238-6630

Finally, there is "Show-Me" Hospitality, a local B&B reservation service offered by the owner of Aunt Sadie's Bed and Breakfast. Specializing in smaller B&Bs, the service offers advice, makes referrals, and books reservations. Phone (800) 348-5210.

CAMPING

Although there are almost four dozen campgrounds within ten miles or so of Branson, only a few offer anything beyond a gravel parking space and minimum hookups. We were amazed, in fact by the lack of shade, landscaping, mountain or water views, and other aesthetic considerations. In general, there is little elbow room, and even less privacy. Tent campers have it even worse, if that's possible.

Fortunately there are exceptions. Our favorites are the Compton Ridge Campground and the Silver Dollar City Campground on Highway 265 overlooking Branson. Both offer larger-than-average shaded sites with nice landscaping and good views. Listed below are these and other area campgrounds that provide a restful, aesthetically pleasing camping environment:

Branson View Campground	(800) 992-9055
Compton Ridge Campground	(800) 233-8648
Cooper Creek Campground	(800) 261-8398
Indian Point Campground	(417) 338-2121
Silver Dollar City Campground	(800) 952-6626
Stormy Point Campground	(800) 933-5175
Table Rock State Park Campground	(800) 344-6946
Acorn Acres Campground	(417) 338-2500
Deer Run Campground	(800) 908-3337

The campgrounds listed above are all about 8–15 minutes from the shows and restaurants of Branson. If you want to camp in Branson, your best bet is the KOA Musicland Kampground, (417) 334-0848. The sites are small, but the campground is shady and well manicured, and best of all, is right in the middle of the action.

Most campgrounds charge a base rate of $15 to $32 per night for a site with a full hookup. If there are more than two people using the site, many operators levy an "Extra Person" charge of $1.50 to $5 per person per night.

Branson area campgrounds, including the less attractive ones, do better with amenities than with aesthetics. The vast majority offer a swimming pool and a necessities store, and some even have restaurants. Most campsites have a picnic table and a lantern holder, and some feature fire rings and/or charcoal grills.

Tent camping seems to be somewhat of an afterthought at most of the campgrounds. For the most part, Branson and the surrounding area are RV territory. For the best tent camping, try the Indian Point Campground operated by the U.S. Army Corps of Engineers, (417) 338-2121, or the Table Rock State Park Campground, (417) 334-4704. A few of the private campgrounds offer nice tent camping sites. These include the Compton Ridge Campground, (417) 338-2911, and the Silver Dollar City Campground, (417) 338-8189. Tent camping sites provide picnic tables, fire rings, and sometimes lantern holders or grills. Restrooms and showers with hot running water are within easy walking distance. Site fees range from $10–14 at the public areas to about $16–18 at the private campgrounds.

One thing to remember if you have your heart set on camping during your Branson trip: weather. If you're going during one of the shoulder seasons, when prices aren't as high but all the shows are still up and running, the weather can be unpredictable. Better to camp when the weather is more reliable than try to save a couple dollars during shoulder season and arrive on a lovely, sunny day only to wake up the next morning to a 20-degree drop in temperature and a rain cloud hovering over your grill.

HOUSEBOATS

Though you would never know it driving along Country Boulevard (Branson's main drag), Branson is surrounded by water on three sides. To the east and south, running past old downtown Branson, is the White River, which forms Lake Taneycomo upstream of the Table Rock Dam. Downstream of the dam to the west of Branson is Table Rock Lake, extending southwest for more than 50 miles.

A fun, scenic, and often economical alternative to conventional lodging in the Branson area is renting a houseboat. Houseboats are air-conditioned and come with fully equipped kitchens. They range in size from cozy models that sleep two or four, to veritable floating condos that sleep up to 16 adults. Rental rates run from $200 a day to $2,200 a week, depending on size and equipment. All marinas renting houseboats provide an orientation cruise where you are taught how to operate the boat. This cruise also provides an opportunity to test all of the boats' systems and equipment.

We recommend eyeballing a houseboat before you rent it. If this is not practical, request that photos of the boat be mailed to you. If you like elbow room and sleeping privacy, rent a boat that sleeps more adults than are in your group. If there are four in your party, for instance, rent a boat that sleeps six or eight. For smaller groups, sailboats are also available.

There are two lakes aurrounding Branson: Lake Taneycomo and Table rock Lake. Lake Taneycomo is more convenient to Branson shows and restaurants than is Table Rock Lake. Table Rock Lake, on the other hand, is much larger and generally more scenic. Because there are no locks at Table Rock Dam, it is impossible to travel by boat from Lake Taneycomo to Table Rock Lake, or vice versa. So don't expect to stay at the more scenic of the two and motor or sail right over to the other lake's marinas to shorten your trip into town.

Following is an abbreviated list of marinas that rent houseboats and/or sailboats:

Table Rock Houseboat Vacations	(417) 335-3042
Tri-Lakes Houseboat Rentals	(800) 982-2628
Branson Marinaplex	(800) 321-9465

Getting a Good Deal on a Room

Most Branson hotels and motels offer a room similar in quality to Holiday Inn or Hampton Inn. The vast majority of Branson's guest-room inventory is five to ten years old, so in general, most rooms are in good repair. Almost all lodging properties offer a pool, and all but a few either have restaurants or are within walking distance of someplace to eat. If you are looking for luxury accommodations, your best bet is to rent a condo.

Because Branson is small, it is easy to get around, except on weekends when bumper-to-bumper traffic clogs Highway 76, the main drag. If you know which shows you want to see, our advice is to choose a hotel close by. During the busier times of the year, you may want to avoid hotels located on Highway 76 unless the property has a back entrance from another road.

Beating Rack Rates

The benchmark for making cost comparisons is always the hotel's standard rate, or *rack rate*. This is what you would pay if, space available, you just walked in off the street and rented a room. In a way, the rack rate is analogous to an airline's standard coach fare. It represents a straight, nondiscounted room rate. In the Branson area, assume that the rack rate is the most you should have to pay and that with a little effort you ought to be able to do better.

To learn the standard room rate, call room reservations at the hotel(s) of your choice. Do not be surprised if there are several standard rates, one for each type of room in the hotel. Have the reservationist explain the difference in the types of rooms available in each price bracket. Also ask the hotel which of the described classes of rooms you would get if you came on a wholesaler, tour operator, or motorcoach package. This information will allow you to make meaningful comparisons among various packages and rates.

Helping Your Travel Agent Help You

In general, travel agents cannot make much money selling trips to Branson or the Ozarks. There are few airfare sales because most people travel to the mountains in their own cars. For the same reason, there is not much business in car rentals. Unless the agent sells a motorcoach tour, a golf package, or the like, he will essentially be relegated to booking your lodging. Since the average stay in Branson is short, this adds up to a lot of work for the agent with little potential for a worthwhile commission. Because an agent derives only a small return for booking travel to Branson and the Ozarks, there isn't much incentive for the travel agent to become product-knowledgeable.

Except for a handful of agents who sell Branson in volume (usually in the area's primary markets), there are comparatively few travel agents who know much about the Ozarks. This lack of information sometimes translates into travelers not getting reservations at the more convenient hotels, paying more than is necessary, or being placed in out-of-the-way or otherwise undesirable lodging.

When you call your travel agent, ask if he or she has been to Branson. Firsthand experience means a lot. If the answer is no, be prepared to give your travel agent some direction. Do not accept any recommendations at face value. Check out the location and rates of any suggested hotel and make certain that the hotel is suited to your itinerary.

Because travel agents tend to be unfamiliar with the Ozark Mountains, your agent may try to plug you into a motorcoach tour or some other preset package. This essentially allows the travel agent to set up your whole trip with a single phone call and still collect an 8–10% commission. The problem with this scenario is that most agents will place 90% of their mountain business with only one or two packagers or tour operators. In other words, it's the path of least resistance for them, and not much choice for you.

To help your travel agent get you the best possible deal, do the following:

1. Determine where you want to stay. This can be accomplished by reviewing the hotel information provided in this guide and by writing or calling hotels which interest you.

2. Check out the Branson and Ozark Mountain travel ads in the Sunday travel section of your local newspaper and compare them to ads running in the newspapers of one of area's key markets. Key markets for Branson include Chicago, St. Louis, Kansas City, Milwaukee, Memphis, Little Rock, Dallas, and Oklahoma City. See if you can find some hotel discounts or packages that fit your plans, and that include a hotel you like.

3. Call the packagers, hotels, or tour operators whose ads you have collected. Ask any questions you might have, but do not book your trip with them directly.

4. Tell your travel agent about what you found and ask if he or she can get you something better. The packages in the paper will serve as a benchmark against which to compare alternatives proposed by your travel agent.

5. Choose from among the options uncovered by you and your travel agent. No matter which option you elect, have your travel agent book it. Even if you go with one of the packages in the newspaper, it will probably be commissionable (at no additional cost to you) and will provide the agent some return on the time invested on your behalf. Also, as a travel professional, your agent should be able to verify the quality and integrity of the package.

No Room at the Inn

If you are having trouble getting a reservation at the hotel of your choice, let your trave agent assist you. The agent might be able to find a package with a tour operator that bypasses the hotel reservations department. If this does not work, he or she can call the sales and marketing department of the hotel and ask them, as a favor, to find you a room. Most hotel sales reps will make a special effort to accommodate travel agents, particularly travel agents who generate a lot of Branson business.

Do not be shy or reluctant about asking your travel agent to make a special call on your behalf. This is common practice in the travel industry and affords the agent an opportunity to renew contacts in the hotel's sales department. If your travel agent cannot get you a room through a personal appeal to the sales department and does not know which tour operators package the hotel you want, have the agent call hotel room reservations and:

1. Identify himself as a travel agent.

2. Inquire about room availability for your required dates; something might have opened up since his (or your) last call.

3. If the reservationist reports there are still no rooms available, have your travel agent ask for the reservations manager.

4. When the reservations manager comes on the line, have your agent identify himself and ask whether the hotel is holding any space for tour operators or wholesalers. If the answer is yes, have your agent request the wholesalers' or tour operators' names and phone numbers. This is information the reservations manager will not ordinarily divulge to an individual but will release to your travel agent. Armed with the names and numbers of wholesalers and tour operators holding space, your agent can start calling to find you a room. To protect yourself, always guarantee your first night with a major credit card (even if you do not plan to arrive late), send a deposit if required, and insist on a written confirmation of your reservation. When you arrive and check in, have your written confirmation handy.

Where the Deals Are

Hotel-room marketing and sales is confusing even to travel professionals. Sellers, particularly the middlemen or wholesalers, are known by a numbing array of different and frequently ill-defined terms. Furthermore, roles overlap, making it difficult to know who specifically is providing a given service. We try below to sort all of this out for you, and encourage you to slog through it, even though room rates in Branson are among the most reasonable to be found. Understanding the system will make you a savvy consumer and will enable you to get the best deals on hotels regardless of your destination.

Tour Operators and Wholesalers

Branson and Ozark Mountain hotels have always had a hard time filling their rooms from Sunday through Thursday. On the weekends, when thousands of weekenders arrive from St. Louis, Kansas City, Memphis, Little

Rock, and Tulsa, the mountains come alive. But on Sunday evening, as the last of the low-landers retreat, the mountains lapse into the doldrums. On many weekdays, even during summer high season, there remain a lot of empty hotel rooms.

Recognizing that an empty hotel room is a liability, various travel entrepreneurs have stepped into the breach, volunteering to sell rooms for the hotels. These entrepreneurs, who call themselves tour operators, inbound travel brokers, travel wholesalers, travel packagers, or receptive operators, require as a *quid pro quo* that the hotels provide them a certain number of rooms, at a significantly reduced nightly rate, which they in turn resell at a profit. As this arrangement extends the sales outreach of the hotels, and since the rooms are going unoccupied, the hotels are only too happy to cooperate with this group of independent sales agents. Though a variety of programs have been developed to sell the rooms, most rooms are marketed as part of motorcoach tours or group and individual travel packages.

This development has been beneficial both to the tourist and the hotel. Predicated on volume, some of the room discount is generally passed along to consumers as an incentive to come to the mountains during the week, or alternatively, to stay longer than a weekend. By purchasing your room through a tour operator or wholesaler, you may be able to obtain a room at the hotel of your choice for considerably less than if you went through the hotel's reservations department. The hotel commits rooms to the wholesaler or tour operator at a specific deep discount, usually 12–25% or more off the standard quoted rate, but makes no effort to control the price the wholesaler offers to his customers.

Wholesalers and tour operators holding space at a hotel for a specific block of time must surrender that space back to the hotel if the rooms are not sold by a certain date, usually 10–30 days in advance. Since the wholesalers' or tour operators' performance and credibility are determined by the number of rooms filled in a given hotel, they are always reluctant to give rooms back. The situation is similar to that of a biology department at a university approaching the end of the year without having spent all of its allocated budget. The department head reasons that if the remaining funds are not spent (and the surplus is returned to the university), the university might reduce his budget for the forthcoming year. Tour operators and wholesalers depend on the hotels for their inventory. The more rooms the hotels allocate, the more inventory they have to sell. If a wholesaler or tour operator keeps returning rooms unsold, it is logical to predict that the hotel will respond by making fewer rooms available in the future. Therefore, the wholesaler would rather sell rooms at a bargain price than give them back to the hotel unsold.

Taking Advantage of Tour Operator and Travel Wholesaler Deals

There are several ways for you to tap into the tour operator and wholesaler market. First, check the travel sections of your Sunday paper for travel packages or tours to Branson. If you cannot find any worthwhile tours or packages advertised in your local paper, go to a good newsstand and buy a Sunday paper, preferably from St. Louis, Memphis, or Chicago, but alternatively from Little Rock, Oklahoma City, Dallas, or Kansas City. These cities are hot markets for Branson, and their newspapers will almost always have a nice selection of packages and tours advertised. Because the competition among tour operators and wholesalers in these cities is so great, you will often find deals that beat the socks off anything offered in other parts of the country.

Tours and travel packages generally consist of room, bus transportation, shows, and occasionally other features such as meals, golf, and admissions to other attractions. Sometimes you can buy a package or tour for any dates desired; other times the operator or wholesaler will specify the dates. In either event, if a particular package fits your needs, you (or your travel agent) can book it directly by calling the phone number listed in the newspaper ad.

Find a tour or package that you like and call for information. Do not be surprised, however, if the advertised package is not wholly available to you. If you live, say, in Pittsburg, a tour operator or wholesaler in St. Louis may not be able to package your round-trip bus to Branson. This is because tour operators and wholesalers usually limit the transportation they sell to round trips originating from their primary market areas. In other words, they can take care of your transportation if you are coming from Oklahoma City or Memphis, but most likely will not have a tour that originates in Pittsburg. What they sometimes do, however, and what they will be delighted to do if they are sitting on some unsold rooms, is sell you the "land only" part of the package. This means you buy the room, shows, and on-site amenities (golf, admissions, etc.), if any, but will take care of your own travel arrangements.

Buying the "land only" part of a package can save big bucks since the tour operator always has more flexibility in discounting the "land" part of the package than in discounting the round-trip transportation component.

One of the sweetest deals in travel is to find a motorcoach tour that is not sold out and buy primo hotel rooms from the operator at his deeply discounted rate.

Room Blocks

Because so many visitors come to Branson on motorcoach tours, the tour operators (as discussed above) reserve large blocks of hotels rooms months in advance for their customers. If the tours do not sell out, and if the remaining rooms cannot be sold to individual travelers, the rooms will be returned to the hotel's available inventory. What this means is that it is sometimes easier to book a room two to three weeks in advance than it is to book a room two to three months in advance, or expressed differently: *keep trying.*

Reservation Services

When wholesalers and consolidators deal directly with the public, they frequently represent themselves as "reservation services." When you call, you can ask for a rate quote for a particular hotel, or ask for their best available deal in the area where you prefer to stay. If there is a maximum amount you are willing to pay, say so. Chances are the service will find something that will work for you, even if they have to shave a dollar or two off their own profit. Sometimes you will have to pay for your room with your credit card when you make your reservation. Other times you will pay as usual, when you check out. Listed below are several services that sell rooms in Branson and the Ozarks:

Branson Memory Tours   A full-service operator that can arrange packages and itineraries for both individuals and groups, including lodging, shows, attractions, sightseeing, meals, and recreation. Call (800) 633-6766 or (417) 338-2534.

Casey's Branson Connection   A full-service receptive operator that books accommodations, arranges packaged tours, reserves show tickets, and provides meals. Serves both consumers and travel agents; call (800) 766-3738 or (417) 335-5933.

Branson Vacation   Obtains reservations for hotels, motels, and condos, as well as shows and attractions. Serves both individual travelers and agents. Call (800) 221-5692. The local phone is (417) 335-8747.

The Room Exchange   A New York–based room consolidator that books hotel rooms throughout the country. Though large cities are their specialty, the Room Exchange can book hotels in Branson. In big cities, the Room Exchange can usually get you a good discount. In the mountains, however,

Hotel and Motel Toll-Free Numbers	
Best Western	(800) 528-1234 U.S. and Canada
	(800) 528-2222 TDD
Comfort Inn	(800) 228-5150 U.S. and Canada
	(800) 228-3323 TDD
Days Inn	(800) 325-2525 U.S.
	(800) 329-7155 TDD
Econo Lodge	(800) 424-4777 U.S.
Fairfield Inn	(800) 228-2800 U.S.
Hampton Inn	(800) 426-7866 U.S. and Canada
	(800) 451-4833 TDD
Holiday Inn	(800) 465-4329 U.S. and Canada
	(800) 238-5544 TDD
Howard Johnson	(800) 654-2000 U.S. and Canada
	(800) 654-8786 TDD
Quality Inn	(800) 228-5151 U.S. and Canada
	(800) 228-3323 TDD
Radisson	(800) 333-3333 U.S. and Canada
	(800) 906-2200 TDD
Ramada Inn	(800) 228-3838 U.S.
	(800) 228-3232 TDD
Residence Inn by Marriott	(800) 331-3131 U.S.
Sleep Inn	(800) SLEEP-INN U.S.
Super 8	(800) 800-8000 U.S. and Canada

owing to the seasonality of demand, discounts on rooms are less certain. Call: (800) 846-7000.

Our experience in Branson and the Ozarks has been that reservation services and packagers are more useful in finding rooms when availability is scarce than in obtaining deep discounts. Calling the hotels ourselves, we were usually able to equal the reservation services' rates when rooms were generally available. On summer weekends, however, when demand was at its highest, and we could not find a room by calling the hotels ourselves, the reservations services could almost always get us a room at a fair price.

Hotel-Sponsored Packages

In addition to selling rooms through tour operators, consolidators, and wholesalers, most hotels periodically offer exceptional deals of their own. Sometimes the packages are specialized, as with show or golf packages, or the packages are only offered at certain times of the year, for instance November and December. Promotion of hotel specials tends to be limited to the hotel's primary markets, which for most properties are Missouri, Arkansas, Oklahoma, Texas, Iowa, Illinois, and Tennessee. If you live in other parts of the country, you can take advantage of the packages, but probably will not see them advertised in your local newspaper.

An important point regarding hotel specials is that the hotel reservationists do not usually inform you of existing specials or offer them to you. In other words, *you have to ask.* Finally, if you are doing your own legwork, and are considering a hotel that is part of a national chain, always call the hotel instead of using the chain's national toll-free number. Quite frequently, the national reservations service is unaware of local specials.

AAA and AARP

Members of the American Automobile Association and the American Association of Retired Persons are eligible for discounts at many of the hotels in Branson and the Ozarks. Call your local AAA office or check the AARP monthly magazine for additional information.

Getting Corporate Rates

Because Branson is primarily a leisure destination, corporate rates are not universally available. Even so, many hotels (especially national chain properties) offer discounted corporate rates (5–20% off rack rate). Usually you do not need to work for a large company or have a special relationship with the hotel to obtain these rates. Simply call the hotel of your choice and ask for their corporate rates. Many hotels will guarantee you the discounted rate on the phone when you make your reservation. Others may make the rate conditional on your providing some sort of *bona fides;* for instance, a fax on your company's letterhead requesting the rate, or a company credit card or business card on check-in. Generally, the screening is not rigorous.

Preferred Rates

In Branson, a preferred rate is a discount made available to travel agents to stimulate their booking activity, or a discount initiated to attract a certain class of traveler. Most preferred rates are promoted through travel industry publications and are often accessible only through an agent.

We recommend sounding out your travel agent about possible deals. Be aware, however, that the rates shown on travel agents' computerized reservations systems are not always the lowest rates obtainable. Zero in on a couple of hotels that fill your needs in terms of location and quality of accommodations, and then have your travel agent call for the latest rates and specials. Hotel reps are almost always more responsive to travel agents because travel agents represent a source of additional business. As discussed earlier, there are certain specials that hotel reps will disclose *only* to travel agents. Travel agents also come in handy when the hotel you want is supposedly booked. A personal appeal from your agent to the hotel's director of sales and marketing will get you a room more than 50% of the time.

Hotels and Motels: Rated and Ranked

WHAT'S IN A ROOM?

Except for cleanliness, state of repair, and decor, most travelers do not pay much attention to hotel rooms. There is, of course, a discernible standard of quality and luxury which differentiates Motel 6 from Holiday Inn, Holiday Inn from Marriott, and so on. In general, however, hotel guests fail to appreciate that some rooms are better engineered than others.

Contrary to what you might suppose, designing a hotel room is (or should be) a lot more complex than picking a bedspread to match the carpet and drapes. Making the room usable to its occupants is an art, a planning discipline which combines both form and function. Decor and taste are important, certainly. No one wants to spend several days in a room where the decor is dated, garish, or even ugly. But beyond the decor, there are variables which determine how "livable" a hotel room is. In Las Vegas, for example, we have seen some beautifully appointed rooms that are simply not well designed for human habitation. The next time you stay in a hotel, pay attention to the details and design elements of your room. Even more than decor, these are the things that will make you feel comfortable and at home.

It takes the *Unofficial Guide* researchers about 40 minutes to inspect a hotel room. Here are a few of the things we check that you may want to start paying attention to:

Room Size   While some smaller rooms are cozy and well designed, a large and uncluttered room is generally preferable, especially for a stay of more than three days.

Temperature Control, Ventilation, and Odor   The guest should be able to control the temperature of the room. The best system, because it's so quiet, is central heating and air conditioning, controlled by the room's own thermostat. The next best system is a room module heater and air conditioner, preferably controlled by an automatic thermostat, but usually by manually operated button controls. The worst system is central heating and air without any sort of room thermostat or guest control.

The vast majority of hotel rooms have windows or balcony doors which have been permanently secured shut. Though there are some legitimate safety and liability issues involved, we prefer windows and balcony doors that can be opened to admit fresh air. Hotel rooms should be odor-free, smoke-free, and not feel stuffy or damp.

Room Security   Better rooms have locks that require a plastic card instead of the traditional lock and key. Card and slot systems allow the hotel, essentially, to change the combination or entry code of the lock with each new guest who uses the room. A burglar who has somehow acquired a room key to a conventional lock can afford to wait until the situation is right before using the key to gain access. Not so with a card and slot system. Though larger hotels and hotel chains with lock and key systems usually rotate their locks once each year, they remain vulnerable to hotel thieves much of the time. Many smaller or independent properties rarely rotate their locks.

In addition to the entry lock system, the door should have a deadbolt, and preferably a chain that can be locked from the inside. A chain by itself is not sufficient. Doors should also have a peephole. Windows and balcony doors, if any, should have secure locks.

Safety   Every room should have a fire or smoke alarm, clear fire instructions, and preferably a sprinkler system. Bathtubs should have a nonskid surface, and shower stalls should have doors which either open outward or slide side-to-side. Bathroom electrical outlets should be high on the wall and not too close to the sink. Balconies should have sturdy, high rails.

Noise   Most travelers have been kept awake by the television, partying, or amorous activities of people in the next room, or by traffic on the street outside. Better hotels are designed with noise control in mind. Wall and ceiling construction are substantial, effectively screening routine noise. Carpets and drapes, in addition to being decorative, also absorb and muffle sounds. Mattresses mounted on stable platforms or sturdy bed frames do not squeak even when challenged by the most passionate and acrobatic lovers. Televisions enclosed in cabinets, and with volume governors, rarely disturb guests in adjacent rooms.

In better hotels, the air conditioning and heating system is well maintained and operates without noise or vibration. Likewise, plumbing is quiet and positioned away from the sleeping area. Doors to the hall, and to adjoining rooms, are thick and well fitted to better keep out noise.

Darkness Control   Ever been in a hotel room where the curtains would not quite come together in the middle? Thick, lined curtains which close completely in the center and which extend beyond the dimensions of the window or door frame are required. In a well-planned room, the curtains, shades, or blinds should almost totally block light at any time of day.

Lighting   Poor lighting is an extremely common problem in American hotel rooms. The lighting is usually adequate for dressing, relaxing, or watching television, but not for reading or working. Lighting needs to be bright over tables and desks, and alongside couches or easy chairs. Since so many people read in bed, there should be a separate light for each person. A room with two queen beds should have individual lights for four people. Better bedside reading lights illuminate a small area, so if you want to sleep and someone else prefers to stay up and read, you will not be bothered by the light. The worst situation by far is a single lamp on a table between beds. In each bed, only the person next to the lamp will have sufficient light to read. This deficiency is often compounded by light bulbs of insufficient wattage.

In addition, closet areas should be well-lit and there should be a switch near the door that turns on lights in the room when you enter. A seldom-seen, but desirable, feature is a bedside console that allows a guest to control all or most lights in the room from bed.

Furnishings   At bare minimum, the bed(s) must be firm. Pillows should be made with nonallergenic fillers and, in addition to the sheets and spread, a blanket should be provided. Bedclothes should be laundered with a fabric softener and changed daily. Better hotels usually provide extra blankets and pillows in the room or on request, and sometimes use a second topsheet between the blanket and the spread.

There should be a dresser large enough to hold clothes for two people during a five-day stay. A small table with two chairs, or a desk with a chair, should be provided. The room should be equipped with a luggage rack and a three-quarter- to full-length mirror.

The television should be color, cable-connected, and ideally have a volume governor and remote control. It should be mounted on a swivel base, preferably enclosed in a cabinet. Local channels should be posted on the set and a local TV program guide should be supplied.

The telephone should be touch-tone, conveniently situated for bedside use. On or near it should be easily understood dialing instructions and a rate card. Local white and yellow pages should be provided. Better hotels have phones in the bath and equip room phones with long cords.

Well-designed hotel rooms usually have a plush armchair or a sleeper sofa for lounging and reading. Better headboards are padded for comfortable reading in bed, and there should be a nightstand or table on each side of the bed(s). Nice extras in any hotel room include a small refrigerator, a digital alarm clock, and a coffeemaker.

Bathroom   Two sinks are better than one, and you cannot have too much counter space. A sink outside the bath is a great convenience when one person needs to dress while another showers. Sinks should have drains with stoppers.

Better bathrooms have both tub and shower with a nonslip bottom. Tub and shower controls should be easy to operate. Adjustable shower heads are preferred. The bath needs to be well lit and should have an exhaust fan and a guest-controlled bathroom heater. Towels should be large, soft, fluffy, and provided in generous quantities, as should hand towels and washcloths. There should be an electrical outlet for each sink, conveniently and safely placed.

Complimentary shampoo, conditioner, and lotion are a plus, as are robes and bathmats. Better hotels supply their bathrooms with tissues and extra toilet paper. Luxurious bathrooms feature a phone, a hair dryer, sometimes a small television, or even a jacuzzi.

ROOM RATINGS

To separate properties according to the relative quality, tastefulness, state of repair, cleanliness, and size of their *standard rooms,* we have grouped the hotels and motels into classifications denoted by stars. Star ratings in this guide apply to Branson and Ozark Mountain properties only and do not necessarily correspond to ratings awarded by Mobil, AAA, or other travel critics. Because stars have little relevance when awarded in the absence of commonly recognized standards of comparison, we have tied our ratings to expected levels of quality established by specific American hotel corporations.

Star ratings apply to *room quality only,* and describe the property's standard accommodations. For most hotels and motels, a standard accommodation is a hotel room with either one king bed or two queen beds. In an all-suite property, the standard accommodation is either a one- or two-room suite. In addition to standard accommodations, many hotels offer luxury rooms and special suites which are not rated in this guide. Star ratings for rooms are assigned without regard to whether a property has a restaurant, recreational facilities, entertainment, or other extras.

Room Star Ratings
★★★★★ **Superior Rooms** Tasteful and luxurious by any standard
★★★★ **Extremely Nice Rooms** What you would expect at a Hyatt Regency or Marriott
★★★ **Nice Rooms** Holiday Inn or comparable quality
★★ **Adequate Rooms** Clean, comfortable, and functional without frills (like a Motel 6)
★ **Super Budget**

In addition to stars (which delineate broad categories), we also employ a numerical rating system. Our rating scale is 0–100, with 100 as the best possible rating, and zero (0) as the worst. Numerical ratings are presented to show the difference we perceive between one property and another. Rooms at the Baymont Inn, Welk Resort Center, and the Barrington Hotel, for instance, are all rated as ★★★ (three stars). In the supplemental numerical ratings, the Baymont Inn and the Welk Resort Center are rated 73 and 71, respectively, while the Barrington Hotel is rated 66. This means that within the three-star category, the Baymont and the Welk are comparable, and both have somewhat nicer rooms than the Barrington.

How the Hotels Compare

Here is a comparison of the hotel rooms in Branson and the surrounding area. We've focused strictly on room quality, and excluded any consideration of location, services, recreation, or amenities. If you use a subsequent edition of this guide, you will notice that many of the ratings and rankings change. These changes are occasioned by such positive developments as guest-room renovation, improved maintenance, and improved housekeeping. Failure to properly maintain guest rooms and poor housekeeping negatively affect the ratings. Finally, some ratings change as a result of enlarging our sample size.

Because we cannot check every room in a hotel, we inspect a number of randomly chosen rooms. The more rooms we inspect in a particular hotel, the more representative our sample is of the property as a whole. Some of the ratings in this edition will change as a result of extended sampling.

Cost estimates are based on the hotel's published rack rates for standard rooms, averaged between weekday and weekend prices. Each "$" represents $40. Thus a cost symbol of "$$$" means a room (or suite) at that hotel will average about $120 a night (it may be less for weekdays or more on weekends).

Finally, before you begin to shop for a hotel, take a look at this letter we received from a couple in Hot Springs, Arkansas:

> *"We canceled our room reservations to follow the advice in your book [and reserved a hotel highly ranked by the* Unofficial Guide]. *We wanted inexpensive, but clean and cheerful. We got inexpensive, but [also] dirty, grim, and depressing. I really felt disappointed in your advice and the room. It was the pits. That was the one real piece of information I needed from your book! The room spoiled the holiday for me aside from our touring."*

Needless to say, this letter was as unsettling to us as the bad room was to our reader. Our integrity as travel journalists, after all, is based on the quality of the information we provide to our readers. Even with the best of intentions and the most conscientious research, however, we cannot inspect every room in every hotel. What we do, in statistical terms, is take a sample: we check out several rooms selected at random in each hotel and base our ratings and rankings on those rooms. The inspections are conducted anonymously and without the knowledge of the property's management. Although unusual, it is certainly possible that the rooms we randomly inspect are not representative of the majority of rooms at a particular hotel. Another possibility is that the rooms we inspect in a given hotel *are* representative, but that by bad luck a reader is assigned a room which is inferior. When rechecking the hotel our reader disliked so intensely, we discovered our rating was correctly representative, but that he and his wife had unfortunately been assigned to one of a small number of threadbare rooms scheduled for renovation.

The key to avoiding disappointment is to do some advance snooping around. We recommend that you ask to be sent a photo of a hotel's standard guest room before you book, or at least get a copy of the hotel's promotional brochure. Be forewarned, however, that some hotel chains use the same guest room photo in their promotional literature for *all* hotels in the chain, and that the guest room in a specific property may not resemble the photo in the brochure. When you or your travel agent call, ask how old the property is and when the guest room you are being assigned was last renovated. If you arrive and are assigned a room inferior to that which you had been led to expect, demand to be moved to another room.

Along with hotels and motels, our list below includes a number of the larger condos and bed-and-breakfasts.

How the Hotels Compare				
Hotel	Room Star Rating	Room Quality Rating	Cost ($=$40)	Phone
Chateau on the Lake	★★★★★	97	$$$$+	(417) 334-1161
Bradford Inn	★★★★½	94	$$–	(417) 338-5555
Branson Hotel B&B	★★★★½	93	$$+	(417) 335-6104
Thousand Hills Golf Resort	★★★★½	91	$$	(417) 336-5873
Big Cedar Lodge	★★★★½	90	$$$–	(417) 335-2777
Sunterra/Plantation at Fall Creek Resort (condos)	★★★★	87	$$+	(417) 334-6404
Surrey Condominiums	★★★★	86	$$+	(800) 714-7710
Village at Indian Point	★★★★	86	$$$–	(417) 338-5800
Pointe Royale Condo Resort	★★★★	83	$$+	(417) 334-5614
Residence Inn	★★★★	83	$$+	(417) 336-4077
Treehouse Condominiums	★★★½	82	$$–	(417) 338-5199
Radisson Hotel	★★★½	80	$$+	(417) 335-5767
Branson Lodge	★★★½	79	$$–	(417) 334-3105
Rock Lane Resort (condos)	★★★½	79	$$$	(417) 338-2211
Sammy Lane Resort (new rooms)	★★★½	79	$$	(417) 334-3253
Still Waters Resort	★★★½	79	$$$+	(417) 338-2323
Copper Tree Suites	★★★½	76	$$+	(417) 335-3233
Fall Creek B & B	★★★½	76	$$	(417) 334-3939
Palace Inn	★★★½	76	$$+	(417) 334-7666
Grand Oaks Hotel (king rooms)	★★★	74	$$+	(417) 336-6423
Hotel Grand Victorian	★★★	74	$$+	(417) 336-2935
Baymont Inn	★★★	73	$$–	(417) 336-6161
Welk Resort Center	★★★	71	$$+	(417) 337-7469
Lantern Bay Resort	★★★	70	$$$–	(417) 338-3000

How the Hotels Compare (continued)

Hotel	Room Star Rating	Room Quality Rating	Cost ($=$40)	Phone
Park Inn	★★★	70	$$–	(417) 336-2100
Grand Oaks Hotel (double rooms)	★★★	69	$$–	(417) 336-6423
Magnolia Inn	★★★	69	$+	(417) 334-2300
Comfort Inn	★★★	68	$$–	(417) 335-4727
The Guest House	★★★	68	$+	(417) 336-3132
The Kings Quarters	★★★	68	$+	(417) 334-5464
Settle Inn	★★★	68	$$–	(417) 335-4700
Trails and Resort	★★★	68	$$–	(417) 338-2633
Bradford on the Lake	★★★	67	$+	(417) 338-2218
Fairfield Inn	★★★	67	$$–	(417) 336-5665
Lodge of the Ozarks	★★★	67	$$	(417) 334-7535
Rock Lane Resort (motel rooms)	★★★	67	$$–	(417) 338-2211
Barrington Hotel	★★★	66	$+	(417) 334-8866
Best Western Music Capital Inn	★★★	66	$$–	(417) 334-8378
Hampton Inn West	★★★	66	$$–	(417) 337-5762
Tara Inn	★★★	66	$+	(417) 334-8272
Cascades Inn	★★★	65	$$–	(417) 335-8424
Copper Tree Suites (rooms)	★★★	65	$$	(417) 335-3233
Foxborough Inn	★★★	65	$+	(417) 335-4369
Hampton Inn (Green Mtn Drive)	★★★	65	$+	(417) 334-6500
Old Matt's Guest House	★★★	65	$	(417) 334-0031
Ozark Regal Hotel	★★★	65	$+	(417) 336-2200
Sunterra/Plantation at Fall Creek Resort (rooms)	★★★	65	$+	(417) 334-6404
Travelers Inn	★★★	65	$$	(417) 336-1100
Best Inns of Branson	★★½	64	$+	(417) 336-2378
Blue Bayou Motor Inn	★★½	64	$+	(417) 334-5758
Branson Inn (new rooms)	★★½	64	$+	(417) 334-5121
Branson Towers	★★½	64	$$–	(417) 336-4500
Classic Motor Inn	★★½	64	$+	(417) 334-6991
Econo Lodge	★★½	64	$+	(417) 336-4849
Fall Creek Inn	★★½	64	$+	(417) 336-6056
Holiday Inn Express	★★½	64	$$–	(417) 334-1985
Howard Johnson	★★½	64	$$–	(417) 336-5151
Mountain Music Inn	★★½	64	$+	(417) 335-6625
Peach Tree Inn	★★½	64	$$–	(417) 335-5900

How the Hotels Compare (continued)

Hotel	Room Star Rating	Room Quality Rating	Cost ($=$40)	Phone
Quality Inn	★★½	64	$$–	(417) 335-6776
Quality Inn (Hwy. 76)	★★½	64	$$–	(417) 334-1194
Ramada Limited	★★½	64	$+	(417) 337-5207
Sleep Inn	★★½	64	$+	(417) 336-3770
Southern Oaks Inn	★★½	64	$+	(417) 335-8108
Vickery Resort	★★½	64	$+	(417) 334-4687
Country Hearth Inn	★★½	63	$+	(417) 334-0040
Grand Country Inn	★★½	63	$+	(417) 335-3535
Harmony Inn	★★½	63	$–	(417) 334-5510
Honeysuckle Inn	★★½	63	$+	(417) 335-2030
Leisure Country Inn	★★½	63	$+	(417) 335-2425
Old Southern Inn	★★½	63	$	(417) 338-2900
The Plantation Inn	★★½	63	$+	(417) 334-3600
Scenic Hills Inn	★★½	63	$	(417) 336-8855
Victorian Palace	★★½	63	$$–	(417) 334-8727
Yellow Rose Motel	★★½	63	$+	(417) 336-3650
Best Western Rustic Oak	★★½	62	$+	(417) 334-6464
Boxcar Willie Motel #1	★★½	62	$+	(417) 334-8873
E-Z Center Motel	★★½	62	$–	(417) 334-8200
The Falls Parkway Inn	★★½	62	$+	(417) 336-3255
Gazebo Inn	★★½	62	$+	(417) 335-3826
Lynina Inn	★★½	62	$	(417) 335-2277
Motel 6	★★½	62	$	(417) 335-8990
Polar Bear Inn	★★½	62	$+	(417) 336-5663
Rosebud Inn	★★½	62	$+	(417) 336-4000
Seven Gables Inn	★★½	62	$+	(417) 334-7077
Whispering Hills Inn	★★½	62	$	(417) 335-4922
Best Western Knight's Inn	★★½	61	$$–	(417) 334-1894
Days Inn	★★½	61	$+	(417) 334-5544
Dogwood Inn	★★½	61	$+	(417) 334-5101
Eagles Inn	★★½	61	$	(800) 728-2664
Expressway Inn	★★½	61	$$+	(417) 334-1700
Fiddlers Inn	★★½	61	$+	(417) 334-2212
Green Gables Inn	★★½	61	$+	(417) 336-3400
Queen Anne Motel I	★★½	61	$	(417) 335-8100
Stonewall West Motor Inn	★★½	61	$+	(417) 334-5173

How the Hotels Compare (continued)

Hotel	Room Star Rating	Room Quality Rating	Cost ($=$40)	Phone
Stratford House Inn	★★½	61	$+	(417) 334-3700
76 Express Inn	★★½	60	$–	(417) 334-7500
Alpine Lodge	★★½	60	$+	(417) 338-2514
Boxcar Willie Motel #2	★★½	60	$+	(417) 336-3837
Dutch Kountry Inn	★★½	60	$+	(417) 335-2100
Edgewood Motel	★★½	60	$+	(417) 334-1000
Lazy Valley Resort (new rooms)	★★½	60	$+	(417) 334-2397
Melody Lane Inn	★★½	60	$+	(417) 334-8598
Atrium Inn	★★½	59	$+	(417) 336-6000
Branson Inn (old rooms)	★★½	59	$+	(417) 334-5121
Cardinal Hill Cottages	★★½	59	$+	(417) 338-8732
Country Western Motor Inn	★★½	59	$	(417) 334-6978
Super 8	★★½	59	$$–	(417) 334-8880
Aunt Mollie's Motel	★★½	58	$	(417) 334-0366
Branson Travelodge	★★½	58	$+	(417) 334-8300
Indian Point Resort	★★½	58	$$$	(417) 338-2250
Rocking Chair Inn	★★½	58	$	(417) 334-2323
Sammy Lane Resort (old rooms)	★★½	57	$$–	(417) 334-3253
Surrey Inn	★★½	57	$$–	(417) 335-5090
Good Shepherd Inn	★★½	56	$–	(417) 334-1695
Hillbilly Inn	★★½	56	$	(417) 334-3946
Indian Trails Resort	★★½	56	$+	(417) 338-2327
Silver Fountain Inn	★★½	56	$+	(417) 334-5125
Ben's Wishing Well Inn	★★	55	$+	(417) 334-6950
Lazy Valley Resort (old rooms)	★★	55	$+	(417) 334-2397

TOP 30 BEST DEALS IN BRANSON

Having compared the guest room quality of hotels, let's reorder the list to rank the best combinations of quality and value in a room. As before, the rankings are made without consideration of location or the availability of restaurant(s), recreational facilities, entertainment, and/or amenities. Once again, each lodging property is awarded a value rating on a 0–100 scale. The higher the rating, the better the value.

We recently had a reader complain to us that he had booked one of our top-ranked rooms in terms of value and had been very disappointed in the room. We noticed that the room the reader occupied had a quality rating of ★★½. We would remind you that the value ratings are intended to give you some sense of value received for dollars spent. A ★★½ room at $30 may have the same value rating as a ★★★★ room at $85, but that does not mean the rooms will be of comparable quality. Regardless of whether it's a good deal or not, a ★★½ room is still a ★★½ room.

Listed below are the best room buys for the money, regardless of location or star classification, based on averaged rack rates. Note that sometimes a suite can cost less than a hotel room.

Top 30 Best Deals in Branson

Hotel	Room Star Rating	Room Quality Rating	Cost ($=$40)
1. Bradford Inn	★★★★½	94	$$–
2. 76 Express Inn	★★½	60	$–
3. Thousand Hills Golf Resort	★★★★½	91	$$
4. Old Matt's Guest House	★★★	65	$
5. Harmony Inn	★★½	63	$–
6. Bradford on the Lake	★★★	67	$+
7. Branson Lodge	★★★½	79	$$–
8. E-Z Center Motel	★★½	62	$–
9. Branson Hotel B&B	★★★★½	93	$$+
10. Old Southern Inn	★★½	63	$
11. Whispering Hills Inn	★★½	62	$
12. Good Shepherd Inn	★★½	56	$–
13. Magnolia Inn	★★★	69	$+
14. Ozark Regal Hotel	★★★	65	$+
15. Scenic Hills Inn	★★½	63	$
16. Rocking Chair Inn	★★½	58	$
17. Sunterra/Plantation at Fall Creek Resort (condos)	★★★★	87	$$+
18. Sunterra/Plantation at Fall Creek Resort (rooms)	★★★	65	$+
19. Treehouse Condominiums	★★★½	82	$$–
20. Surrey Condominiums	★★★★	86	$$+
21. Queen Anne Motel I	★★½	61	$

	Top 30 Best Deals in Branson (continued)		
Hotel	Room Star Rating	Room Quality Rating	Cost ($=$40)
22. Lynina Inn	★★½	62	$
23. Residence Inn	★★★★	83	$$+
24. Country Western Motor Inn	★★½	59	$
25. Big Cedar Lodge	★★★★½	90	$$$−
26. Eagles Inn	★★½	61	$
27. Aunt Mollie's Motel	★★½	58	$
28. Pointe Royale Condo Resort	★★★★	83	$$+
29. Tara Inn	★★★	66	$+
30. Hampton Inn (Green Mtn Drive)	★★★	65	$+

Part Three

Getting In, Getting Around

Arriving

BY AIR

Branson is in the southwest corner of Missouri, about 45 miles south of Springfield on US 65 and close to the Arkansas border. There is a small airport, M. Graham Clark Airport at College of the Ozarks, just outside the city, though it's for private-airplane use only.

Otherwise, unless you're taking a bus tour or driving the entire way, you'll probably have to fly into Springfield and rent a car. There are shuttle services and taxis you can charter between Springfield and Branson, but the rates range from $45 to $50 one-way, and then you'll still be shuttle-dependent when you get to Branson.

TWA, Northwest, and United all have some commuter service into Springfield, and most of the major car rental chains, including Avis, Hertz, Budget, and National have counters there. The Springfield airport is fairly small, and the rental car parking lots are within easy walking distance. Though you can check baggage at the counter, most seasoned commuters check their bags plane-side and pick them back up when they step off.

No matter which rental company you choose, however, this is not one of the times to economize. Even though it's a short and well-marked trip into Branson, we urge you *not* to rent a compact or subcompact car. There are long, slow grades for a substantial length of the highway (and in a few areas around Branson as well). If you are underpowered, you will not only struggle to avoid holding up traffic behind you, but you will also negate the lower daily rental rate by going through your gasoline at an astonishing pace. In summer, when air conditioning is pretty important, you'll find the acceleration to be even tougher.

The Ozarks and Surrounding Area

N

BY ROAD

Most folks drive their own cars to Branson, or alternatively arrive in a chauffeured bus. Either way, US 65 is the main access route. It's about 50 miles north on US 65 to Springfield, and another 167 miles along various highways to Kansas City. St. Louis is 220 miles northeast of Springfield via I-44. Southeast of Branson is Little Rock, about 170 miles distant. The closest interstate highways are I-44, which runs northeast from Oklahoma City to St. Louis, going through Springfield on the way, and I-40, running all the way from Wilmington, North Carolina to Barstow, California, passing about 140 miles south of Branson as it crosses Arkansas. Missouri Highway 76, Branson's main drag, intersects US 65 about 12 miles north of the Missouri/Arkansas state line.

We recommend following US 65 south from Springfield into town if possible, since the smaller roads leading in, though they may look more direct on a map, are twisty-turny affairs that may leave you white-knuckled, and are frequently under construction. It is well worth jogging around from the southern states to avoid US 65 between Little Rock and Branson. We suggest you follow I-55 north to US 60 west.

Getting Oriented

We recommend that you devote the first couple of hours to getting the lay of the land—and to getting accustomed to the slow pace of driving in Branson. Actually, if you are coming from Springfield, you will probably run into construction and two-lane traffic quite a while before getting into town. Although it's one of the roads being widened, US 65 has a notorious 20-mile stretch that is two lanes wide and hilly.

US 65 runs north/south and is a four-lane, limited-access highway at Branson. There are two Branson exits, Missouri Highway 248 to the north, and Branson's main drag, Missouri Highway 76.

West Highway Missouri 76 is also called Main Street (especially in old Downtown Branson) or 76 Country Boulevard or "the Strip," and more than 20 of the theaters, along with several of the bigger malls and novelty attractions, are on MO 76. There are so many, in fact, and they sprouted up so fast, that most addresses are descriptive rather than specific. The Grand Palace, for instance, advertises that it's "located on 76 next to Andy Williams' Moon River Theater." This is why nearly every brochure, hotel room advertiser, and entertainment guide includes a map with the attractions marked as little stars or red dots. You pretty much have to find one theater in relation to another.

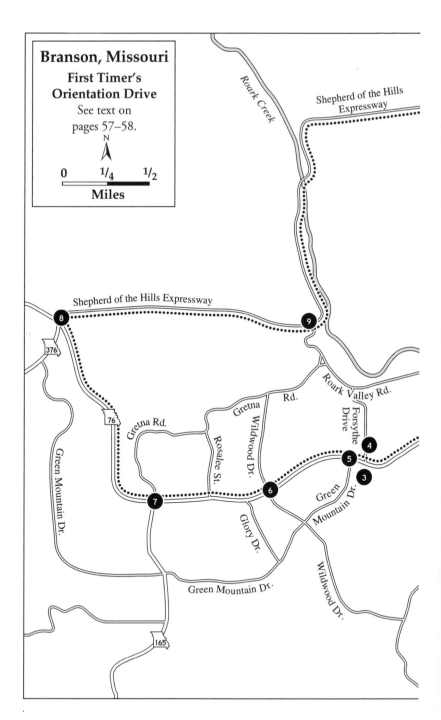

Branson, Missouri

First Timer's Orientation Drive

See text on pages 57–58.

N

0   1/4   1/2

Miles

Roark Creek

Shepherd of the Hills Expressway

Shepherd of the Hills Expressway

8

9

376

76

Roark Valley Rd.

Gretna Rd.

Gretna Rd.

Rosalee St.

Wildwood Dr.

Forsythe Drive

4

5

3

6

Green

Mountain Dr.

7

Glory Dr.

Green Mountain Dr.

Green Mountain Dr.

Wildwood Dr.

165

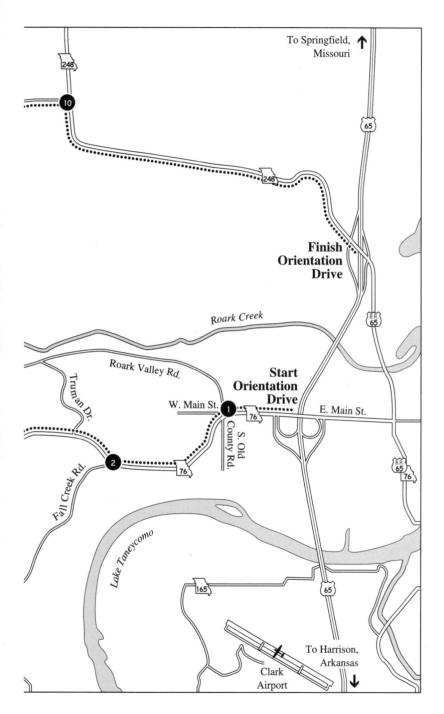

Highway 76, the Strip, is about five miles long from the beginning to the end of the theater district, and maybe five more miles west to Silver Dollar City. Along that westerly section of 76 are also the other two theme parks, Branson USA and Shepherd of the Hills.

Since MO 76 is the oldest part of the Strip, and the theaters and motels are so closely jammed together, many of the newer (larger, fancier) venues are a little farther out. Shepherd of the Hills Expressway is the secondary theater and motel strip, north and, for a while, parallel to 76. It runs from *Country Tonite!* past Shoji Tabuchi and ends more or less at Mel Tillis. From there, MO 248 loops back to Kirby Van Burch and US 65. The last big show route is MO 165, which heads due south from the Osmonds to Lawrence Welk and on to Table Rock Lake and the showboat *Branson Belle.*

First Stop: Branson Chamber of Commerce Visitors Center

If you are driving in on US 65, the first thing you should do is get off at the Route 248 West interchange, one junction north of MO 76, and pull into the Chamber of Commerce Visitors Center, just west of the overpass. If you are driving on Highway 13, which also runs between Springfield and Branson (and is more convenient for those wanting to stop at Bass Pro Outdoor World), there is another Chamber office just north of the exit for 265/76 which heads east toward Branson by way of Silver Dollar City and Shepherd of the Hills park. Pick up any brochures you didn't get and any "latest" map showing the secondary roads, which are essential to getting around. Branson is a town in flux. Do take care to request the latest map, and don't just rely on the one printed in the brochure you happened to pick up. Also ask for one of the color-coded road maps which will help with the short-cut systems we refer to frequently. If you don't have a motel reservation, use their search-a-room computer. (We don't actually recommend your leaving the room till last, but maybe it was an impulse trip.)

Pick out one of the area maps that's big and blank enough to mark on and keep it open. Ideally, hand it to whoever's in the passenger seat. Now, get back on 65, drive south another mile, and take the Main Street/MO 76 West exit off MO 65 and head west. The minute the ramp curves around—it turns a full U, so you'll want to turn left at the light—you'll begin to see souvenir shops and motels. You'll also probably begin to see the traffic. If you didn't stop at the tourist information center above, there is a smaller one across MO 76 from the ramp.

FIRST-TIMER'S ORIENTATION DRIVE

With your map of Branson, drive west on MO 76 from its intersection with US 65, making the circuit described below. Note the important intersections and landmarks, and annotate your map as indicated below. If you have time, explore the streets running north and south off 76. When the traffic gets bad (and it will), these side streets will serve as your escape routes. By driving the circuit, you will get an idea of how attractions are clustered, and it will be easier to understand the shortcuts we'll mention, using theaters as signposts. This is also a good time to get into the spirit of letting other cars turn in front of you and letting pedestrians cross. You'll have to slow your pace in Branson, so you may as well start now.

1. *Roark Valley Road*　Heading west on 76 from US 65 you'll see Roark Valley Road turning north (the light just mentioned); it's one of the biggest and most direct shortcuts to Shepherd of the Hills Expressway and also to Gretna Road (another useful back route).

2. *Fall Creek Road*　Continuing west on 76 about a mile farther, you'll hit the intersection of Fall Creek Road. Lightly developed but four lanes wide, it cuts southwest to MO 165 near the Lawrence Welk Complex. You can bypass the busy middle part of the 76 Strip by cutting southwest on Fall Creek Road, turning right (north) on 165 and rejoining 76 just before it curves to the northwest. Mark the Fall Creek Road and MO 76 intersection with a big X on your map.

3. *Wal-Mart*　A little west of Fall Creek Road on 76, notice the Wal-Mart on the left; a lot of locals give directions that include the store.

4. *Forsythe Street*　Opposite Wal-Mart is Forsythe Street, which provides an escape route north off 76 to Roark Valley Road.

5. *Green Mountain Road*　Continuing on 76 west of Wal-Mart, look for Green Mountain Road, which cuts off to the south, crosses the intersection with Wildwood Drive, and intersects with 165, and continues on to 376. Several of the restaurants and newer motels are located on Green Mountain Road.

6. *Wildwood Drive*　This intersection—Wildwood and 76, marked by the Blue Velvet, Moon River, and Grand Palace theaters—

should be marked with an X as the central crossroads on your map. (That's another fun thing about Branson; the map has a beat, and you can dance to it.) Wildwood runs north to Gretna Road (which connects to Roark Valley Road) and south to Green Mountain Road, and below that to Fall Creek Road.

7. *Missouri Highway 165/Gretna Road Intersection*   Farther west on 76, the traffic light just past the Osmond Family Theater at MO 165 is another good landmark. (Note that if you turn south here, you will be on MO 165. If you turn north, MO 165 is called Gretna Road.) Just beyond the 165 intersection, 76 curves northwest.

8. *Shepherd of the Hills Expressway*   Another couple of miles west on 76 brings you to the major intersection of Shepherd of the Hills Expressway, the third big X to mark on your map. Turn right here.

9. *Roark Valley Road Intersection*   About a mile and a half down Shepherd of the Hills Expressway, past the purple Shoji Tabuchi palace, is a three-way traffic signal. Remember this intersection. Roark Valley Road jogs south across Gretna Road and then swings wide back to the very east end of Highway 76, back where you started.

10. *Completing the Loop*   For the time being, though, continue straight on Shepherd of the Hills, bearing left along the old rail-road tracks and up the hill to one of the newest areas of town. The huge white Tara of a theater on your right is The Grand Mansion. Keep going over the rise and back down to where the road runs into Missouri Highway 248. From here, look left—Mel Tillis is just up the road—but turn right. About two miles along you'll see the entrance to the Kirby Van Burch and Wayne Newton theaters on the left, the Chamber of Commerce build-ing on the right, and the ramps back onto US 65. Congratula-tions! You've made the circuit.

If you're really into orienteering, you can quickly go back down 65 and this time head east on 76 to Old Downtown Branson and the riverfront; but there's no particular trick to that, so unless you're just curious, it can wait.

RIDE THE DUCKIE ROUND THE KNOBS

Even if you take the driving tour, you probably ought to sign up for one of the sightseeing tours or trolley rides. You'll get a sense of where the outlying attractions are and how close, glimpse the beaches and lake areas, get a little history, and probably hear some pretty bad jokes. If you have joined up with a bus tour or some other packaged vacation, you'll probably get a sightseeing round as part of your package.

All the sightseeing tours offer a good itinerary, but unless the weather is really bad, we recommend you "Ride the Ducks." Ducks (from the military DUKW) are amphibious motor vehicles originally used in World War II. The Ducks tour is particularly good if you're interested in the construction and modification of tanks, Jeeps, and the like, because the Ducks route includes a private drive through the company's open-air "museum" of retired military machinery. For more details, see Part Six, "Theme Parks, Museums, and Other Attractions."

The advantage of the Ducks over other tours is that they travel both on land and in water, and the trips include a pleasant few minutes on Table Rock Lake. And to be honest, the wackiness of the Ducks tours and their "captains" is a good introduction to the expansiveness that is an integral part of the Branson experience.

GETTING AROUND WITHOUT A CAR

If you don't want to drive at all, but want to wander farther than your feet will take you, there are taxis and shopping trolleys along major routes. A-OK Shuttle and Tours, for example, runs from the various hotels (also "clustered," incidentally) to the theme parks, theaters, shopping centers, etc., but shuttles are not free ($5 one-way, $8 round-trip) and reservations are usually required. For more information call (417) 334-8687.

Part Four

Getting Along in Branson

The Etiquette of Branson:
Mind Your "Please" and Queues

There is little formal protocol in Branson—there is little formal anything in Branson—and what there is can be summed up in six words: "Stay in line" and "Let someone in." These are more important than you may think.

Almost everything in Branson requires standing in line, from picking up tickets to eating at the buffets to driving the two-lane road that is the Strip. This is democracy, Branson-style; and it works pretty well. Knowing that lines are long, those in them try to be pleasant—they strike up conversations, hold places for those who need to go to the bathroom, and so on. When it comes to the traffic, it works the same way, which many visitors from big cities find especially astonishing. If you are on foot and need to cross the street, just stand on the curb a moment: if the first driver doesn't stop and wave you over, the second will (the third at the utmost). Similarly, if you're driving and you pull up from a side street to the main highway, put your turn signal on and wait calmly; you'll be invited in. There is a particular rhythm to these exchanges, so please remember to wave or say "Thank you." Otherwise, everybody feels somehow shorted.

With this hospitality comes responsibility, of course. When you are in the main line of traffic, you will be expected to let cars in, pedestrians cross, etc. The center lane of Highway 76 is only for immediate turns. There are signs, incidentally, warning you not to use the center as a through lane, and it's one of the regulations the local constabulary takes most seriously. This apparently "wasted" lane seems odd to some urbanites. One journalist, writing about Branson for *GQ* magazine, actually complained because so many people observed the traffic patterns that she didn't have much opportunity to jump into the center lane and pass them.

Oddly, there seems to be a little less unanimity about restroom etiquette. The lines hold (unless somebody begs), and small children are made room for. But there seems to be some confusion about whether to clean up after oneself (yes, always) or whether to tip the attendant if there is one. So far, at least, the restroom staff in Branson (and only a few theaters even have them yet) do not actively assist visitors by passing them towels, cosmetics, etc., so you need not leave a tip unless you want to. And, of course, only if there is a tip jar visible.

Incidentally, "bladder matters," one of the *Unofficial Guide*'s most appreciated insights when discussing theater venues, usually takes up a small section in our books; but in this case, there's not much reason to worry—at least in terms of quantity. Branson is widely equipped—so widely, it's occasionally over-extented. Restaurants, hotel lobbies, theaters, shops, etc., all have easy-to-locate restrooms. However, again we remind you that not all are wheelchair accessible, so plan accordingly.

SMILE, AND THE WORLD . . .

The other surprisingly important thing to remember is to smile. Smile "Howdy," smile "Thanks," smile "I'm having a good time." It's not only good for you, it's good public relations. People respond better, volunteer more information, and bring the coffee pot around a little faster.

Do not take this old-fashioned courtesy lightly. It's part of the general sense of returning to Middle America that characterizes a lot of the Branson experience. And if you either abuse or ignore other people's friendly overtures, they often have a tendency to take extreme offense. Then everybody's mood gets ruined.

Having made the passing acquaintance of your waitress/bartender/parking lot attendant/hotel receptionist, make sure to use them as a resource. Ask them about the new shows, the new theaters; if they haven't seen everything in town, they've sure heard from people who have. Also, residents know everything about getting from place to place without using the main drag and about the quieter "locals'" bars and hangouts, etc.

As an aside, many of the waiters, bartenders, and other people you'll meet in town are part-time performers or self-appointed ambassadors of good will. Locals, you will discover, are very anxious for you to have a good time, and will offer extensive personal insights and opinions, often unsolicited. This is one of the great charms of Branson, and you should expect to have more in the way of conversations with "strangers," i.e., Bransonites, than you may be used to. If you're introverted or excessively formal, you may be in for a shock.

Finally, show a little imagination. So much of Branson life centers on the theaters that the generally simultaneous showtimes also affect the various restaurants and shopping centers in town, not to mention traffic. Tour groups and buses tend to deliver guests to restaurants almost simultaneously, and the hosts and bartenders and so on can get run pretty ragged. Try to avoid these rush hours altogether. If, however, you can't eat later, or, like us, enjoy people-watching, we suggest you smile sympathetically at the mixmaster and say, "Take your time, I'm not in a hurry." You'll not only win their appreciation, but you're also apt to get a little extra with your order when it comes.

WHAT TO WEAR AROUND TOWN

As we noted above, almost nothing is formal in Branson, and that goes double for clothing. A very few restaurants may ask men to wear sports jackets, but ties are considered displays of individuality. You see more bolos and string ties than four-in-hands, and almost no bow ties other than the black ones on Andy Williams and polka-dots on the occasional red-nosed clown.

Women need not wear dresses, either, although occasionally ladies at the later-night dance club put on a flounce or two. It's hard to compete with the performers, anyway, who routinely upend established custom by wearing sequins before noon and white boots in winter.

Basically, pack a wrap suitable to the season, and otherwise dress to be comfortable. This is especially important if you are with a tour group, since that probably means you'll be on and off the bus, in and out of restaurants, and toting the odd souvenir. Remember that Branson entertainers are commercial professionals as well; while Louise Mandrell may not actually hawk her Shopping Network cosmetics from the stage, all the stars pretty shamelessly dangle tour jackets, T-shirts, key rings, videos, and recordings, especially at intermission.

There is one piece of your wardrobe that does deserve careful consideration, and that's your shoes. Unless you are young, going dancing, going to one of the fancier restaurants, or in a show yourself, wear flat, supportive shoes *with tread.* Real walking shoes would be the best, though any kind of sneaker, athletic shoe or orthopedic sole will do. Many of the parking lots are steeply slanted, and so are the aisles and carpets inside some of the theaters. Traffic and parking are such that we recommend you try to plan some of your excursions as park-and-walks, meaning that you leave your car at a central location and visit several attractions without moving it ("clustering"), so you'll be curving up and down a bit with the sidewalks. And of course, if you plan to visit one of the theme parks or amusement centers or factory outlet malls, you'll definitely want the sole support.

WHAT TO WEAR (THE INSIDE STORY)

We do have a few clothing tips, however: wear elastic or loose waistbands if you're planning to make the buffet circuit. In Branson, Sansabelt golf pants are practically a uniform. It seems to be a human genome problem that nobody has ever learned how to undereat when faced with the phrase "all you can"—even when you know you'll be faced with another buffet in five or six hours—so you might as well dress for excess. (You might consider carrying Alka-Seltzer, gas tablets, or Beano, too; that sort of forethought can save you a lot of distracting discomfort, not to mention embarrassment.)

Carry a bag with shoulder straps so you don't have to clutch it while examining T-shirts and cassettes. If you are going to a theater and want to wear shorts, longer, Bermuda-cut shorts are better, because some of the theaters, the older ones especially, have sturdy and slightly rough upholstery designed to last through a lot of thighs. The upholstery also plays havoc with stockings; you can check the individual theater descriptions, but as a general rule, we'd suggest you wear either heavy-duty tights or forget the hose altogether.

Remember that you'll probably be using a lot of public restrooms, and standing in line again, so avoid jumpsuits with zippers you can't reach, tricky wrap or pin outfits, or ornate suspenders you might drop (another reason to skip the stockings). And quite honestly, we suggest you give up on the cutesy extra-brief, thong, or power pushup underwear, too; not only will you be squirming in your seat, but everybody else in the theater will, too.

Either wear long sleeves that you can roll up and down or carry a light wrap in the summer, because the theaters and restaurants are air-conditioned and you'll be sitting still for two hours or more. Besides, if you do insist on wearing shorts, at least you'll have something to put between you and that horsehair upholstery.

THE LITTLE THINGS

There are also a few things you can do to make other people's visits more pleasant, and hope they do unto you as well. For example, if you do buy a snack at the concession stand, don't wait to unwrap it or do the noisy tearing stuff as the show starts. Either eat it in the lobby or at least rip it open there. Don't wad up crackly paper when you're through and toss it around.

If you do smoke, don't stand right outside the theater door so that non-smoking patrons have to pass through a cloud to get in. Walk 30 feet into the parking lot before lighting up.

If you wear a hat (and with all the warnings about sun exposure, more and more people do), please remember that even baseball and farmer's caps stick out into somebody's view line, not to mention anything with a real brim or crown.

Children are welcome in Branson—they insist on your spending a lot of money—and as noted, are allowed into most shows either at a lower price or for free. However, there are times not to take the kids, either because the theater doesn't have a "time-out room," or because the show is unlikely to hold their attention, or because they're already tired and cranky. Don't push your luck: there are a couple of babysitting companies in town, and your hotel staff can get you the names.

And if you're with an early-rising tour group, try to walk softly down to the hotel lobby. Thanks.

SEEING THE LIGHT

Photographing the stars is Branson's number one spectator sport, even more than getting autographs. But "photograph" is quite specific: most theaters forbid both video cameras and audio recorders of any sort. Violators are subject to ejection and possibly confiscation of the camera or recorder. So don't bring anything other than a still camera.

More importantly, don't walk into town with a year's supply of flashbulbs. Flashbulbs are a fan's least useful expense. Not only do they *not* do your photographs any good, they probably blind the performers and annoy other helpless audience members. This is absolutely true: even if you are within five feet of a star, right there at the foot of the stage, your instamatic flash is not going to provide any greater illumination than the stage lighting—not to mention the spotlights that follow the star from side to side. In fact, you're more likely to overexpose the picture and wind up with the ghost of Jim Stafford instead.

If you are up in the balcony or in the back of the room, it's entirely useless; no flashbulb reaches beyond about 12 feet at best. You're only blinding your neighbors. If you don't believe us, read the directions about when to use your flash. Or get a book on photography for beginners. Again, the stage lighting will provide plenty of what's called "available light"—you'll get dramatic, professional-looking photos just using those spotlights.

At least respect those signs at various shows specifically saying, NO FLASH PHOTOGRAPHY, PLEASE and the announcers who repeat it. Flashbulbs are a double discourtesy in those cases (not that it seems to stop many people).

Instead of a cheap flashing instamatic, we suggest you try either a moderately priced automatic camera, which will make the adjustments for you, or even try out one of those wide-angle Kodaks. They'll take great stage shots.

Part Five

Entertainment: Theaters and Shows

Preparing Your Game Plan

From time to time, we refer to two concepts or tricks to help you plan your visit. "Cramming" is tight booking of shows during a single day, covering three and maybe even four performances. (Two is almost mandatory if you want to accomplish anything at all.) "Clustering" is the phrase we use for choosing theaters and attractions that are close together, so that you can reduce travel time and general mental wear and tear. We'll show you a few samples a little later in this chapter. Ideally, you can combine both techniques into the optimum entertainment-per-hour scheme, depending on your level of fitness, as the health magazines would say.

Because the hard truth is, unless you have (1) several weeks to spend; (2) imperturbable good humor; and (3) incredible stamina, you cannot see everything Branson has to offer. Trust us on this. The *Unofficial Guide* team has all of the above *and* strong ankles, and we barely made it. After all, there are more than three dozen theaters (most with more than one show) and several more seemingly always under construction, two theme parks, boat cruises and railway rides, tours, and game parks—not to mention the shopping, golfing, bungee-jumping, fishing, and so on. So the first thing to do is settle on which kind of attractions, and how many, you want to enjoy.

That's where we at the *Unofficial Guide* think we can make your vacation better. There are dozens of other lists of attractions in Branson, but not so many critical opinions. Throughout this book, we'll tell you what we really think. We'll be funny, we'll be frank, but we'll be fair. Our "Overall Ratings" take into account as much of the whole experience as possible: the style and look of a show, the quality of the performance, the predictability of the songs, the creativity of the sets, etc. More than that, we'll give you a sense of the *atmosphere* of each theater, not just the comfort of the seats, the view lines, the sound quality, and so on, but the intangibles that may affect your enjoyment (and that of the other members of your party).

Only the venues that host sit-down concerts and variety performances are rated in this chapter. In Part Six, "Theme Parks, Museums and Other Attractions," we will profile the two theme parks, Silver Dollar City and Shepherd of the Hills, which combine some music and amusement rides into family attractions. Shepherd of the Hills also hosts live outdoor theatrical performances at night, based on the book of the same name; and Silver Dollar City has an after-hours musical variety performance that is included in the park admission.

In the next chapter, we'll also describe the cruise ship attractions (which went up to four with the opening of the *Branson Belle* Showboat in 1995), the Scenic Railway, the Stone Hill Winery, the museums (Hollywood Wax, Ripley's Believe It Or Not! and others), the Waltzing Waters display, IMAX theater, White Water amusement park, etc.

BETWEEN THE LINES

Every show in Branson is family-safe, but some shows are more entertaining for whole families than others. In our individual theater and show profiles, we will point out those performances more likely to hold the attentions of small children or teenagers. (Teens, as we pointed out in the introduction, can feel they've fallen into Branson's generation gap unless you pick out a few special attractions.) The pace of a performance needs to be a little faster to keep young children interested, but older audiences prefer a more leisurely rhythm. Parents with infants or toddlers should look under the "Special Features" for what are called "time-out" rooms, glass-fronted rooms in the rear where crying or nursing children can be taken care of without the parents' missing the show. These booths are fitted with speakers so that the show can be heard inside, but not the children outside; they're more likely to have been built into the newer venues.

Similarly, though many performers include songs from the big band and World War II eras, not all are as persuasive or polished as, say, the Lawrence Welk Orchestra. The flip side of that coin is the ten-year-old "Star Search" candidate who sings with video precision but no perception of broken hearts and blighted lives. So we may also refer in the show descriptions to a "reality check" that suggests whether a performer seems really dedicated to presenting his material freshly, whether it seems cheap or slick or smarmy or whether the material and the musician are well matched. The ten-year-old may rate high on kids' interest rating or even "grandparents appeal," but low on the reality-check scale.

RATINGS AND RANKINGS

We urge you to read through the profiles, because we do pay so much attention to the little things; but for your convenience in making some of the basic decisions, there is an immediate rating you can glance at, called the "Overall Ratings." These start at one star, for a perfunctory performance, and go up to four stars for the best in town. Anything less than one star probably won't last a whole season, anyway. As a shortcut, we have listed the four- and three-and-a-half-star shows below. We also mark some as "Best Bargains," shows that not only rate three or four stars but pack a lot of entertainment punch for the money, and a few "Super Savers," extra-discount or package deals. Even so, we urge you to read the profiles before making final choices: If you want comedy mixed in with the music, a straight concert, four stars or not, won't satisfy you.

The "handicapped access" listing takes into account the driveway, lobby, and seating access as well as the restrooms. A "fair" handicapped access rating means there may be some initial difficulty in getting in or limited wheelchair seating, but the show can be seen in relative comfort. It will mean the restrooms are wheelchair accessible, however; any venue that does not have renovated restrooms will have a "No" access rating. (Again, buildings are constantly being upgraded, so you may want to double-check.)

Finally, we'll try to point up good entertainment bargains, and bad deals as well. We realize that not everybody's musical taste is the same, but we think everybody wants to know who works the hardest, who cares the most about the audiences, and who's just going through the motions. After that, as they say on TV, it's your money—it's your choice.

Four-Star Shows   Dino Kartsonakis; the *Lennon Brothers Breakfast Show* (Welk Stage Door Canteen); the Osmond Family show; and *The Promise*.

Three-and-a-Half-Star Shows   The Duttons, Kirby Van Burch, Jim Stafford, Shoji Tabuchi, Mel Tillis, the *Lawrence Welk Show*, and Andy Williams.

SHOWS BY SHOWPLACE

Branson's major musical entertainment can be divided into four categories: celebrity venues, variety and production shows, theatrical performances, and novelty attractions—comedy, magic, etc. We list all the major shows by category below, along with a category for "revue venues," which are stages or rental halls that host three or four different shows, sometimes with overlapping casts, during the course of the day. Since many performers take off either Sunday or Monday (or both), we've listed the theaters that are open on Sundays. We've also listed shows that include meals—breakfast, lunch or dinner—as another useful factor in schedule "cramming."

However, once we get into the detailed individual profiles, attractions are listed by *theater,* which is frequently, but not always, the same as listing them by performer. We do this for several reasons—most importantly, because that is how the local guides and weekly handouts list them, and we want to reduce confusion.

Also, some of the "name" theaters are actually home to more than one celebrity: Wayne Newton does play his own theater, of course, but only in selected months; the rest of the time the Lowe Family of Utah and the Chinese Acrobats are in residence. The Grand Palace is Star Central: Kenny Rogers owns a share and frequently performs there, but it's also where the visiting celebrities such as Reba McEntire or Vince Gill play. Sunday nights at the Palace are almost always a guest night. In the "celebrity" list, therefore, if a performer makes regular appearances in a venue that does not include the star's name, we have put his or her regular theater in parenthesis so you can cross-reference.

What's in a Name?

When the theater does have a "star" name, whatever else is in the title, it's alphabetized under the performer's last name: The Andy Williams Moon River Theater is under "W" in our list, Jennifer's Americana Theater is under "J." That way you don't have to memorize the whole name. The one exception is the Lawrence Welk Champagne Theatre, which, although it obviously doesn't star Welk himself, does host the otherwise apparently immortal cast of the old *Lawrence Welk Show,* complete with Lennon Sisters, Jo Ann Castle at the piano, etc., so we've listed it under "W" as well.

The other (non-celebrity) venues are alphabetized from the front end; i.e., the Grand Palace and 76 Music Hall are under "G" and "S," respectively.

We also list shows by venue because, since you will probably have to make some choices between performers you would like to see but who are all scheduled for the same times, the virtues or drawbacks of the particular venue may be decisive. And a few theaters host three or more different shows a day. However, whenever a theater is primarily used by one performer, particularly one of the major celebrities, we have tried to supply a review of the show as well.

Finally, we rated the theaters first, and the shows second, because frankly it's a lot more common to have the stars and the names change than to have the buildings change. The Remington Theater debuted as the Five Star Theater, and had two more name changes before arriving at its current name.

The Ray Stevens Theatre became *Country Tonite!*, etc. There are renovations going on all the time, and building sales that give the phrase "musical chairs" a whole new meaning: Moe Bandy's theater used to be Jim Stafford's until Stafford bought and rebuilt the place next door. The current Mel Tillis complex is his third home since he moved to town in 1990: he started off by moving into what had been Shoji Tabuchi's place until Tabuchi built the purple palace, then when Tillis moved out, Willie Nelson moved in for a couple of years, then when Tillis moved again, Charley Pride filled in until building . . . well, you get the idea. Consequently, a few venues that we profiled here will probably have changed names or closed—and a few will have opened—since we were there, but we've got your major bets covered.

Please note that although some of the ticket prices listed in the theater profiles include tax, many do not; there is no consensus about that in Branson yet. The additional tax amount is not exorbitant, usually between $1 and $2, but for a whole family, the amount might make a budget difference. Be sure to ask specifically when purchasing tickets.

Please also remember that these schedules are the general rule, and tend to change slightly during the holiday season and the slow period in August (the second two weeks particularly). Performers frequently take on special concert commitments or special appearances elsewhere. Be sure to be very specific about dates and performers, and always inquire about the theater's refund policy in case of a last-minute scheduling change.

SHOWS BY CATEGORY

Celebrity Shows   Moe Bandy, Dino Kartsonakis (Grand Mansion), Mickey Gilley, the Platters, Ronnie Prophet, Tony Orlando, the Osmonds, Jim Owen, Wayne Newton, Kenny Rogers, Jim Stafford, Shoji Tabuchi, Mel Tellis, Bobby Vinton, the Lawrence   Welk Show, Andy Williams, Jennifer Wilson and the Oak Ridge Boys.

Variety and Production Shows   *The Baldknobbers Jamboree, Country Tonite!, Dixie Stampede,* the Duttons, Doug Gabriel, Hughes Brothers, Lowe Family of Utah, *The Presleys' Country Jubilee,* Radio City Music Hall Rockettes, Showboat *Branson Belle,* and Buck Trent.

Theatrical Productions   *The Promise, Two from Galilee, and the Shepherd of the Hills.*

Novelty Shows   Acrobats of China, Broadway on Ice, Cirque Lumiere, Elvis and the Superstars, Legends in Concert, Yakov Smirnoff, Kirby Van Birch, and Phillip Wellford.

Revue Venues Breakfast with the Classics, 50s at the Hop, Lost in the 50s, 76 Music Hall, Sons of the Pioneers, and Starlite Kids.

Breakfast Shows Breakfast with the Classics, Breakfast with Buck Trent, Hughes Brothers, the Lennon Brothers (Welk Stage Door Canteen), and the Showboat *Branson Belle.*

Lunch Shows The Showboat *Branson Belle,* and the Lawrence Welk Show.

Dinner Shows Dixie Stampede, the Platters, the Showboat *Branson Belle,* and the Lawrence Welk Show.

Gospel Shows Braschler Music Show, Barbara Fairchild, *The Promise,* and Two from Galilee.

CLUSTERING AND CRAMMING

You can limit the frustration level and enjoy more of Branson if you either concentrate on small areas or travel in outer circles. The amusement parks and the 76 Mall are pretty much whole-day projects in themselves; but otherwise you may want to hold a mood, suit the age of your group, or just take it easy. Here are a few possible groupings to use as guides:

A Taste of the World Tour You might have to look a little harder but we guarantee that this will expand your expectations of down-home-country Branson USA. This tour also lends a fabulous overview of Branson as it circumnavigates Highway 76. Start at 9 a.m. with Yakov Smirnoff at his What a Country Theater then have lunch at Shogun on Highway 248. Catch the Acrobats of China at the Wayne Newton Theater at 3 p.m. before diving into some savory Italian fare at the Pasta Grill on Green Mountain Road. Finish with Shoji Tabuchi at 8 p.m. in his exquisite purple theater. (For swift movers, an early evening dinner cruise on the *Polynesian Princess* can replace the Acrobats show and Pasta Grill. It sails at 5 p.m. and returns shortly before 7:30, so to make Shoji you almost have to sprout wings.)

A Kids'-Interest Sampler A *Sammy Lane* Pirate Cruise in the morning (four start times before noon); check out the magic at Kirby Van Burch's Theater at 2; followed by some time at the IMAX theater, the White Water or neighboring amusement parks; and Jim Stafford at 8—all, except for the cruise, right in the same neighborhood.

A Nostalgia Special *Lennon Brothers Breakfast Show,* followed by shopping in Old Downtown Branson (take Green Mountain to the east end of

76) and a ride on the Branson Scenic Railway; lunch at the Branson Cafe (six kinds of pie, each with a meringue higher than the next); then one more brief drive back to Bobby Vinton at 3, and a souvenir-buying cruise of the Grand Village shops until the 7 o'clock dinner show with the Platters at the Hughes Brothers Celebrity Theater.

The Cram-Bam-Thank-You-Ma'am Deluxe Arrive at the Branson Mall Music Theater at 8:30 a.m. to assure the enjoyment of your meal before Breakfast with the Classics. Grab a burger and a malt for lunch at the Starlite Diner as you amble your way to the 2 p.m performance at the Dutton Family Theater. Make tracks for your 4:30 departure on the Showboat Branson Belle's dinner cruise. Don't worry, you'll have time to catch your breath before Dino's 8 p.m. show at the Grand Mansion.

The Upscale Cluster Andy Williams and the Grand Palace, with shopping at the Grand Village next door and meals at either McGuffey's (in the parking lot between the two theaters) or the safari-room/flambé-flourish of Buckingham's in the Palace Hotel on the other side of the Village.

The Low-Key Cluster Off the Beaten Track *The Lawrence Welk Show* at 2 and a dinner cruise on the showboat *Branson Belle.*

The Late Starter Mickey Gilley's cafe, Gilley himself at 8, and dancing at the Club Celebrity nightclub next door at Lodge of the Ozarks (Hughes Brothers Celebrity Theater).

The Off-76 Trick There are a couple less-tight clusters that require cars but bypass major traffic jams. For instance, start with Ronnie Prophet at 9:30, then to Shoji Tabuchi at 3, go a block west on Shepherd of the Hills Expressway to the IMAX, take a quick left onto 76 to the Waltzing Waters, and then double back to your left again alongside the Factory Merchants outlet mall to Gretna Road and The Promise Theater or go out Shepherd of the Hills Expressway to Mel Tillis, or Kirby Van Burch's Theater.

The Cowboy's Delight Breakfast with Buck Trent at The Dinner Bell Restaurant at 8, lunch at the Lone Star on Green Mountain Drive (where you may be able to slip into the half-hourly line dance); head back over to 76 for the *Country Tonight!* 3 p.m. show; slip down Truman Road for dinner at the Outback Steak and Oyster Bar, which combines a restaurant and bar with a very upscale clothier and bungee jump (ahem); then west on Highway 76 for the Moe Bandy show at 8. Finish the night with a beer and another line dance at Mesquite Charlie's at the intersection of Gretna and Roark Valley roads.

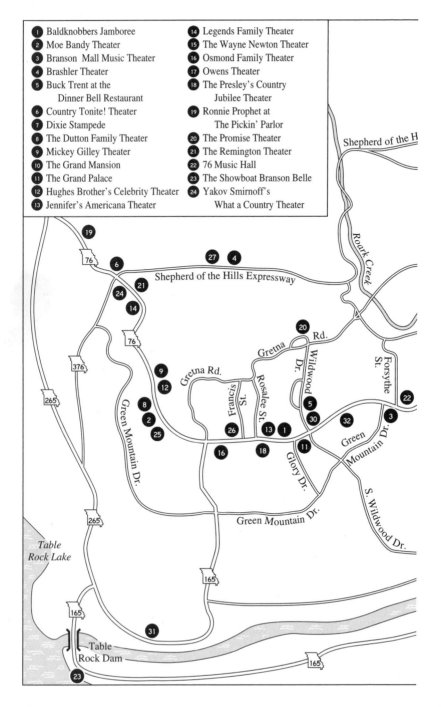

1. Baldknobbers Jamboree
2. Moe Bandy Theater
3. Branson Mall Music Theater
4. Brashler Theater
5. Buck Trent at the
   Dinner Bell Restaurant
6. Country Tonite! Theater
7. Dixie Stampede
8. The Dutton Family Theater
9. Mickey Gilley Theater
10. The Grand Mansion
11. The Grand Palace
12. Hughes Brother's Celebrity Theater
13. Jennifer's Americana Theater
14. Legends Family Theater
15. The Wayne Newton Theater
16. Osmond Family Theater
17. Owens Theater
18. The Presley's Country
    Jubilee Theater
19. Ronnie Prophet at
    The Pickin' Parlor
20. The Promise Theater
21. The Remington Theater
22. 76 Music Hall
23. The Showboat Branson Belle
24. Yakov Smirnoff's
    What a Country Theater

Shepherd of the H

Roark Creek

Shepherd of the Hills Expressway

Gretna Rd.

Gretna Rd.

Wildwood Dr.

Forsythe St.

Francis St.

Rosalee St.

Green Mountain Dr.

Green Mountain Dr.

S. Wildwood Dr.

Glory Dr.

Green Mountain Dr.

Table
Rock Lake

Table
Rock Dam

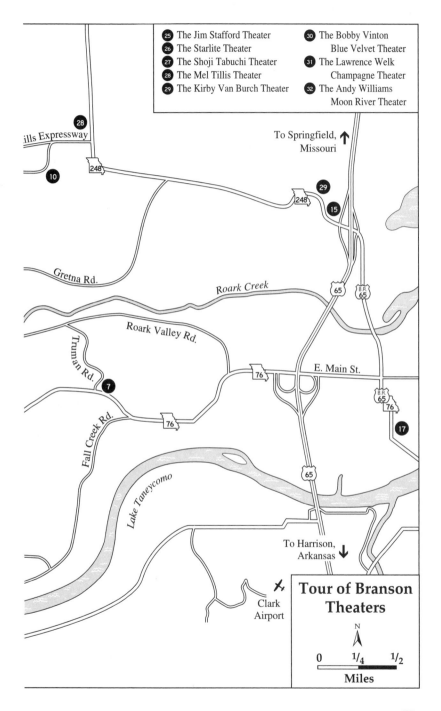

25 The Jim Stafford Theater
26 The Starlite Theater
27 The Shoji Tabuchi Theater
28 The Mel Tillis Theater
29 The Kirby Van Burch Theater

30 The Bobby Vinton
   Blue Velvet Theater
31 The Lawrence Welk
   Champagne Theater
32 The Andy Williams
   Moon River Theater

To Springfield,
Missouri

ills Expressway

248

10

248

29

15

Gretna Rd.

Roark Creek

65

B.R.
65

Roark Valley Rd.

Truman Rd.

7

E. Main St.

76

B.R.
65 76

17

Fall Creek Rd.

76

Lake Taneycomo

65

To Harrison,
Arkansas

Clark
Airport

**Tour of Branson
Theaters**

N

0   1/4   1/2
Miles

Celebrity Showcases

The most famous theaters, of course, are the celebrity palaces, where the stars perform 12 or 13 shows a week in the comfort of their own routines. Since most of these performers now live in Branson full time, they continue to expand their seasons. Most shows have performances pretty much year-round, with breaks around Christmas (although some have special Christmas and even New Year's programs). Dino Kartsonakis, the closest thing to a country/gospel Liberace, has for several years staged elaborate family pageants, complete with costumed production numbers and lavish special effects, simply called Dino's Christmas Extravaganza, now complemented with a year-round presence—both shows at the Grand Palace.

However, even the star palaces range remarkably in size and facilities. In general, of course, the newer they are, the nicer and also the larger they will be. In the course of his theater-building career in Branson, Mel Tillis has graduated from several hundred seats to 2,700. The Grand Mansion has 3,000 seats and the Grand Palace holds 4,000. Even the restaurants are expanding: the Dixie Stampede, a dinner attraction, is something like a cross between an outdoor barbecue and Buffalo Bill's Wild West Show, holds a thousand people, and does away with silverware, too.

Again, we remind you that although most of the celebrities perform in their own theaters on a regular and predictable basis, things do change, not just from season to season but week to week. Ask the Chamber of Commerce staffers if old theaters have closed or changed hands, and if the map you are using to locate the theaters is current. Branson is on the move in more ways than one, and if a theater location shift causes you to arrive late, seating you after curtain inconveniences everyone. When buying tickets, always double-check that no "guests" are performing instead; or if you are planning to see a show in one of the big venues with rotating entertainment such as the Grand Palace, get very specific information on the schedule. This is another good reason to consider contacting the theaters yourself and just making a reservation instead of using a ticket vendor; if you discover that somebody you don't particularly want to see has been inserted into the schedule, you can always benignly ignore your reservations. If you do go through a ticket service, you should probably ask if they have any guarantees or refunds or other adjustments.

The Baldknobbers Jamboree

Location   2835 W. Highway 76, just west of Wildwood

Open   March through mid-December

Type of Show   Music-comedy variety revue

Showtimes   Monday–Saturday, 8 p.m. (warm-up show 7:15)

Ticket Prices $20 adults; $10 children ages 11 and under; season passes $60

Reservations and Information   (417) 334-4528; www.baldknobbers.com

Dark   Sundays

Seating Capacity   1,700

Disabled Access   Fair

Overall Rating   ★★★

General Description   Just about the only indication left of this theater's original incarnation as a skating rink is its low, wide seating and straight-forward views of the elevated stage. The lobby is clean, simple, and attractive; the auditorium has pleated wall fabric "buttoned" with sconces. The staff is exceptionally helpful. Lights and sound equipment are newly renovated and extremely good without being obtrusive. The seats provide medium leg room; the upholstery is coarse but not too rough.

The Show   *The Baldknobbers Jamboree* dates back to 1959, and encompasses three generations of the Mabe family—"family" being a word you'll see a lot of in this context—and a musical director who began at 17 as a banjo prodigy and is still playing keyboards 30 years later. The Jamboree mixes some very Old-Opry style humor, including a couple of sad-sack hillbilly clowns in overalls and droopy drawers and plenty of outhouse jokes, with solid picking and singing. Old-timey musical numbers include washboards and tub bass; newer hit covers show off a strong electric band. Many of the performers double in other shows around town, almost as a piece of tradition: the original Baldknobbers played the role of the original Bald Knobbers in the first productions of *The Shepherd of the Hills,* and also portrayed the gunfighters and street musicians at Silver Dollar City.

However, more than many of the other long-running troupes, the Mabes have allowed their show to "grow up" with the family, so that it seems both more natural and more engaging than some of the more labored old-fashioned shows. The newest addition to the show is the talented Cassandra Butler. She added her voice to the cast during the Baldknobbers 40th Anniversary show. The male romantic idol is Dennis Mabe, who wears desperado-style black leather; and there are two of the standard back-up singers in white boots. Good appeal to all ages; children will especially enjoy the warm-up Ragtime Joe's piano and audience participation games. *Reality check:* Extremely hard-working cast, talented and sincere, with good variety in the show and not too many gimmicks.

Moe Bandy Theater

Location　3446 W. Hwy. 76, between Gretna Road and Shepherd of the Hills Expressway

Open　Mid-March through December

Type of Show　Celebrity headliner

Showtimes　Tuesday through Sunday, 8 p.m.

Ticket Prices　$21 adults; children 12 and under free

Other Shows on Site　Sons of the Pioneers

Showtimes　Tuesday through Sunday, 2 p.m.

Ticket Prices　$19 adults; children 12 and under free

Reservations and Information　(417) 334-5333; (888) 3BANDY4, www.moebandy.com

Dark　Mondays

Seating Capacity　700

Disabled Access　Good

Overall Rating　★★★

General Description　This plain, unpretentious theater suits the show well. The stage is rigged for television-type backdrop changes and is just wide enough to allow dramatic spotlight vignettes. Updated in 1999, the theater now features a state of the art video system, along with brand-new special effects.

The Show　Many of Moe Bandy's fans believe him to be one of the great honky-tonk singers of the late 70s and early 80s. Taking off from his hit record "Americana," which is also the name of his band, he plays a fair amount of patriotic music in his show, lightened by some laughter courtesy of comedian Hargus Marcel and the Houdini-like escape acts of magician Anthony Zappa. Bandy is a pleasant rather than charismatic entertainer, but he gets a high reality check. Greatest age appeal is to middle adults and some seniors—limited children's draw.

Other Shows　This is a musical tribute to old-timey cowboy country music. It is performed in the spirit of the late Roy Rogers, who was the last of the original Sons of the Pioneers. Songs include "Red River Valley," "Timber Trail," "Don't Fence Me In," "Tumbleweeds," and "Happy Trails to You."

Branson Mall Music Theater

Location　2206 W. Hwy. 76, between Wal-Mart and Consumer's

Open　April through December; limited shows January through March

Type of Show　Nostalgic review of times past

Showtimes   May through mid-December, 2 and 8 p.m.

Ticket Prices   Adults $22.25; children ages 6–11 $8.50

Other Shows on Site   Breakfast with the Classics

Showtimes   Tuesday through Sunday, 9:30 a.m.

Ticket Prices $17.50 adults; children under 12 free; $5 extra for all ages for breakfast

Reservations and Information   (417) 335-5300

Dark   Mondays, also some Tuesdays and Wednesdays

Seating Capacity   750

Disabled Access   Good

Overall Rating   ★★★

General Description   As the name suggests, this venue is located right in the middle of a strip mall. Opening comments to both shows find the emcee touting it as "the only musical venue in the world sharing wall space with Wal-mart!" Fortunantly, passing by the ticket booth into the gift shop does begin to change your mood, and by the time you are seated in the auditorium, the fact that you are in a shopping center is long forgotten. The seating is divided parallel to the stage by a walking aisle at about row 25, and the middle sections are flanked by left and right wings. *Tip:* The blue seats from row 25 to the back are much newer (and much more comfortable), but beware of the two ceiling-support poles in the back middle section just waiting to block views from certain seats. If you can bear to sit in the worn yellow seats in the front sections, though, it makes for a much more interactive show, with the acoustics and view being much better.

The Show   This 50s-style review is unmatched by other like-shows in town. Nedra Culp's dynamite voice shows just why she was voted Branson's Female Vocalist of the Year, with her ability to belt out Tina and Aretha.

The Morning Show   Tributes to the great music of past generations performed by powerful voices and big band instruments are so convincing that you would think you were listening to Tony Bennett, the Inkspots and the Andrews Sisters themselves. The fast songs bring you to the edge of your seat, while the slow songs relax you and take you back to the day . . . . At no point is the entertainment dull or canned. The performers actually rely on their talents in this show, making the viewer realize how overproduced some of the other shows in Branson are. *Tip:* Give yourself enough time to wake up and comb your hair before wandering in for the show— for you will be reappearing on countless VCR's. The shows are taped daily (cast and audience) and are for sale as soon as the show ends, so that you can literally buy the show you've seen.

Braschler Theater

Location   3044 Shepherd of the Hills Expressway

Open   May through mid-December; limited dates in April

Type of Show   Country gospel

Showtimes   8:30 p.m.; Thursday gospel matinee 2 p.m.

Other Shows on Site   Barbara Fairchild

Showtimes   Late April through mid-December; Monday–Saturday pre-show, 9:30 a.m.

Ticket Prices   All shows: adults $19.50 including tax; children under 12 free

Reservations and Information   (417) 334-4363; www.barbarafairchild.com

Dark   Friday nights

Seating Capacity   700

Disabled Access   Excellent

Overall Rating   ★★½

General Description   Perched on a small rise off of the Shepard of the Hills Parkway sits the Braschler Theater on rather level ground. Persons who require the use of a wheelchair will find this a welcome change to Branson's otherwise steep and unyielding terrain. The theater's façade is reminicscent of a southern Baptist church including classical white columns and steep pitched roof. The small lobby, decorated in quaint country Victorian, hosts concessions and an open gift shop of collectables and like-styled gifts. You may find this area a bit crowded during intermission as patrons vie for a snack, restrooms, or a look at a souvenir. You enter the auditorium from either of two spacious aisles and by one cross-aisle. The seats are new and very comfortable. There is no balcony to dampen sound or support poles to block views. *Tip:* When traveling to or from this theater, using the Gretna and Roark Valley Roads is a wise way to cross-cut gridlocked Branson traffic!

The Show   The ambience of the building's façade prepares you for exactly what you'd expect, an enjoyable presentation of country, western, and southern gospel music and an occasional contemporary Christian song or two. Cliff Braschler, patriarch of the show, leads this ensemble of talented musicians and vocalists while stenciled lighting effects twirl about the schrim at the back of the stage. Audiences delight at the harmony and rich blend of the Braschler Quartet. Different members showcase their talents and instruments. *Tip:* During intermission, take the opportunity to walk down and meet the musicians. They always welcome meeting the audience personally.

Breakfast with Buck Trent at the Dinner Bell Restaurant

Location   118 Hampshire Drive, behind the Bobby Vinton Theater off North Wildwood

Open   Mid-April through December

Type of Show   Country and bluegrass musical variety show

Showtimes   Monday–Saturday, 9 a.m.

Ticket Price $16 adults; children under 12 are free; breakfast package $19; breakfast for children $2.50

Reservations and Information   (417) 334-8839; www.bucktrent.com

Dark   Sundays and some Saturdays

Seating Capacity   400

Disabled Access   Good

Overall Rating   ★★½

General Description   Located inside the Dinner Bell Restaurant, the banquet table arrangement affords a suprisingly good view from any seat. The stage is small and barely elevated, and the ceiling is so low that the drummer and back-up guitarists seem to get lost in the shadows from time to time. However, the overall sound quality is very full and clear, and the lighting of the production is soft and unobtrusive. Breakfast is quite tasty and served family-style, with large dishes of eggs, bacon, and fried potatoes placed on each table. The food is served promptly at 8 a.m., is removed at five until nine, and is well worth the minimal extra charge.

The Show   Buck Trent is the name, face, and cement of this show. However, the talent lies in the rest of his cast, with outstanding energy, high enthusiasm, and top-notch ability. Wade and Bruce, the fiddlers two, keep the crowd on the edge of their seats, cheering and laughing. Beverly Cotton Dillard picks the banjo beautifully, and in an amazing, old-timey clawfoot style. Trent plays a number here and there, but seems to exist mainly for song and mood transitions—which he does by attempting to pass off some really bad one-liners for jokes. This is moderately distracting from the flow of the otherwise crowd-pleasing performance. There is not much kid appeal here, but those in the older crowd will definitely leave with smiles on their faces and two thumbs up!

Country Tonite! Theater

Location   4080 W. Highway 76 at Shepherd of the Hills Expressway

Open   March through mid-December

Type of Show   Music-comedy variety revue

Showtimes   Friday–Wednesday, 3 and 8 p.m.

Ticket Prices $23.50 ages 12 and up; $11 children ages 4–11; ages 3 and under in parent's lap free

Reservations and Information   (417) 334-2422 or (800) GO-TONITE; www.countrytonite.com

Dark   Thursdays

Seating Capacity   2,000

Disabled Access   Excellent

Overall Rating   ★★

General Description   This building is only a few years old, and clearly belongs in the "second generation" of facilities: the wide, curving lobby swings from the gift shop and double-sized concession stand around to (ramped) aisles. The seats are divided into two main sections by a transverse aisle, and the lighting booth is in the center of the "risers," or second bank of seats. The stage is barely elevated, and the show is pretty much a straight-ahead production. However, the arena is more narrow than some, so nearly all seats face the stage anyway. Seating itself is good, with wide elbow room, good leg room, and fairly smooth upholstery unlikely to threaten your skin. Good stereo sound, fairly basic lighting.

The Show   This is one of those "variety" revues that march in a lot of cutesy stage children, many of whom have either over-developed, canned Whitney Houston voices or underdeveloped vocal cords and precocious concepts of charm. *Reality check:* It makes your throat hurt.

   The other part of the show, which was perhaps only a third, featured some "professional" cover singers, very smooth and oddly bloodless; some fairly impressive back-up singers doing the Branson two-step, and a dozen or so dancers/cloggers. This is obviously supposed to have broad family appeal, but it doesn't always work: older patrons seem put off by the brassy kids, and other kids don't seem to find it very inspiring, either. Two bad signs: a very low flashbulb quotient, and a smaller second-half crowd..

Dixie Stampede

Location   1525 W. Highway 76, just west of Roark Valley Road

Open   March through December

Type of Show   Dinner show

Showtimes   Daily, 5:30 p.m.; pre-show at 4:40 p.m.

Ticket Price $39 adults; $22 children ages 4–11; free for lap children under 4 eating off parent's plate

Reservations and Information   (417) 336-3000 or (800) 520-5544; www.dixiestampede.com

Seating Capacity   1,000

Disabled Access   Good

Overall Rating   ★★★

General Description   This Dollywood production is a sort of combination picnic, horse show, and *Gone With the Wind* operetta. Beginning at 7, the "Dixie Belle Saloon" serves (nonalcoholic) drinks and live western entertainment; then you're seated behind multi-tiered U-shaped—make that horseshoe-shaped—counters facing a dirt floor. The meal is dished out from big trays at your seat, and eaten without utensils, thus making cleanup easy and reducing the noise. The menu includes smoked ribs and roasted chicken, soup, corn on the cob, "Dixie Bread" and a potato, plus dessert and coffee, tea, or Pepsi.

The Show   There is some trick ridin' and trick ropin', parasol twirlin' and hoop skirt swirlin', and a bit of very Buffalo Bill–style derring-do with runaway horses and covered wagons. A mini Blue-and-Gray skirmish tops it off, with patriotic climax and special lighting effects. The main show is 90 minutes long. A special Christmas show will replace the Tara mansion with a four-story gingerbread house and "elves."

Kids' interest is very high. Year 2000 sees the start of a new pre-show, which will feature those beloved racing pigs and ostriches. Also, the three dozen or so horses and other animals are just waiting to perform!

Dutton Family Theater

Location   3454 W. Hwy. 76, just west of Gretna Road

Open   Late April through December

Type of Show   Music variety

Showtimes   Monday through Saturday, 2 and 8 p.m. (limited 10 a.m. performances)

Ticket Prices   Adults $19.50; children ages 12 and under free

Reservations and Information   (417) 332-2772; (888) 388-8661

Dark   Sundays

Seating Capacity   900

Disabled Access   Good

Overall Rating   ★★★½

General Description   This theater is about as old-fashioned and barebones as a theater gets—a stage with standing amplifiers and microphones, and a little curtaining here and there. It is oddly reminiscent of a high school auditorium in the early 70s. However, this somehow lends a cozy and real sense to the heart-felt performance issuing from the stage. Since the show is not over-produced and the stage is only three and a half feet above the ground, the closer you are, the better. *Tip:* The seats are old and a little too soft, with limited leg room—request a seat on or close to the aisle. Also, if you are tempted by the caramel corn sold at the concession stand, please eat it before you enter the theater. It is amazing how much the clear plastic that it is in crackles.

The Show   The Duttons are truly a spectacular family. The talent, showmanship and feeling within each one of the members is evident from the opening of the first curtain. Talk about a too-good-to-be-true story of accomplishment! While father, Dean, was working as a professor of economics for a major university, mother Sheila was busy raising their seven children. As a lesson in discipline and music appreciation, each child began a study of classical violin between the ages of three and five. As they got older, the children started a bluegrass band of their own. In search of a bass player, they (finally) convinced Sheila to pick up a musical instrument for the first time in her life, at age thirty-seven. Dean's guitar completed the family ensemble and in the fall of 1991, he took a "one-time" semester leave from teaching so the family could have the experience of touring in what was projected as a "modest" schedule.

Almost 2500 concerts later, this extraordinary family now has a permanent home in Branson at the former Boxcar Willie Theater. The show opened the night before Boxcar gave up his battle with leukemia. His endorsement of the Dutton family praised their efforts, claiming "We had lots of acts to choose from, but we think the Duttons can fill the shoes you have supported throughout the years. The show is a good, clean, family show, and I know everyone will be pleased with them."

Two special qualities have become hallmarks of the Duttons performances: versatility and the ability to establish an immediate rapport with their audiences. Their versatility allows them to switch seamlessly back and forth between folk, country, and bluegrass to formal attire and classical music by such greats as Handel and Bach. Not only are they skilled violin, banjo, cello, and mandolin players, they sing, clog, yodel, and know how to put huge grins on their audience's faces.

The Mickey Gilley Theater

Location   3455 W. Highway 76, between Gretna Road and Shepherd of the Hills Expressway

Open   Mid-March through mid-December

Type of Show   Music-comedy concert

Showtimes   Saturday–Thursday, 8 p.m.

Ticket Prices $23 adults; $5 children ages 4–12; ages 3 and under in parent's lap free

Other Shows on Site   *The Jim Owen Morning Show*

Showtimes   Saturday–Thursday, 10 a.m.

Ticket Prices $17 adults; $6 children ages 12 and under

Reservations and Information   (417) 334-3210; www.gilleys.com

Dark   Varies

Seating Capacity   950

Disabled Access   Good

Overall Rating   ★★★

General Description   This is a nice but neat theater, with something of the same intimate feel that across-the-street neighbors Jim Stafford and Moe Bandy emphasize, only in a Southwest-influenced turquoise and sand style. The gift shop is modest and bridges the gap between Gilley's Texas Cafe across the parking lot (see restaurant listings) and Gilley's own low-key persona: bottles of barbecue sauce and salsa, designer denim clothing, fireplace tools, and black-and-white "cow licks"—novelty headgear.

The Show   Mickey Gilley's show gets its rhythm from his personality: simultaneously rollicking and relaxed, a sort of laid-back chaos. There's a hint of that Saturday night/Sunday morning roadhouse-and-church–service ambiguity in his stage persona: when you hear him wind up, you'll remember that his cousins are Jerry Lee Lewis and Jimmy Swaggart. His honky-tonk vocals are well-backed by the Urban Cowboy Band.

The Morning Show   Jim Owen is best known for his performances as Hank Williams in two movies and a TV video as well as on stage; it's still the material closest to his heart. (The Last Cowboy Band is a sort of local pickers' collective.) However, he's also written songs for other stars, which he plays. The Sunshine Express is a trio of what they call in the business "girl singers" which specializes in old 40s and 50s harmonies. *Tip:* Arrive at 9:15 for free coffee and doughnuts.

The Grand Mansion

Location   187 Expressway Lane, west of the intersection of Shepherd of the Hills and Hwy. 248

Open   April through October

Type of Show   Musical variety

Showtimes   Daily, 3 and 8 p.m. (depending upon performer)

Ticket Prices   Varies

Reservations and Information   (800) 884-4536; www.thegrandmansion.com

Dark   Varies

Seating Capacity   3,200

Disabled Access   Good

Overall Rating   ★★★★

General Description   Over three thousand seats, premium sound, and one of the largest stages in Branson make the Grand Mansion a superb place to spend an evening. This exquisitely beautiful theater, formerly called the Magical Mansion has been acquired by the same people that own the Grand Palace. We found the two venues, though quite separate, to be quite confusing. Similar names, somewhat similar appearances and the engagement of the same performers at different times can boggle the mind.

The Show   Dino's "Music for All Time" extravaganza, with its lavish costumes, big production numbers, and lots of flash makes the world seem a little less dreary. At ease with his cavernous audience, Dino makes his way through popular hits on Liberace's Baldwin grand piano covered in more than 100,000 mirror tiles. Full of smoke and laser fire, Dino's productions also have some quiet moments when his solo playing holds intimate sway over the house. A touch of magic here and there is a nice, added dimension.

The Grand Palace

Location   2700 W. Highway 76 at Wildwood Drive, just west of Andy Williams Moon River Theater

Open   April through mid-December

Type of Show   Music concerts, variety venue

Frequent Headliners   The Oak Ridge Boys; George Jones; Charley Pride; LeAnn Rimes; The Radio City Music Hall Rockettes; Kenny Rogers

Showtimes   Monday–Saturday, 8 p.m.

Ticket Prices   Variable, generally $35–$50

Discounts   AAA, AARP

Reservations and Information   (800) 884-4536 or (417) 339-5700; www.thegrandpalace.com

Dark   Sundays

Seating Capacity   4,000

Disabled Access   Excellent

Overall Rating   ★★★★

General Description   The builders of the Grand Palace spent $13 million to live up to the name, packing the walls with ceramic tile, wall sconces, velvet curtains and a lobby with grand staircase and chandelier that would do San Simeon proud. A million dollars of that went to state-of-the-art acoustical equipment and lighting (including a whole bank of lasers and "fireworks") which are designed to make the Palace TV-friendly; it's already hosted several specials. The one drawback to its production-style sound is that even the best live music can seem canned when it has to be channeled through the microphones and back out the speakers, but most audiences, inured to TV and radio sound already, don't mind.

The stage itself is theatrical in height and sweep, with a slight curve out into the audience and a high ceiling that allows for a lot of very professional scene-changing and special effects—including Louise Mandrell "flying" in on a parachute. Despite the large number of seats, they are wide, with good leg room and support; and thanks to the careful balcony design, no seat is farther than 120 feet from stage front. However, although the stars do move from side to side allowing photos from all angles, shows do primarily face front, so do avoid the very back outside corners.

Tip: The extravagant productions here, up to and including the Rockettes, draw even more than the usual number of walk-up photographers, so the closest aisle seats are frequently, if temporarily, obscured. It would be best to avoid the five rows in the very front.

The best views are downstairs about halfway back and upstairs all around the front ten rows. However, the Grand Palace has tiered ticket prices to match the seats; if you have no problems seeing or hearing, you may be quite happy with the less expensive upper balcony seats. Note that there is no elevator, so wheelchair users must get downstairs tickets. And oddly for such a new and family-friendly venue, there is no "time-out" room in the rear. *Tip:* The rear parking lot slopes but there is quite a bit of flat-surface parking in front of the theater and some more at the Grand Village shopping center next door; see some of the suggestions in the "Clustering and Cramming" section.

Special features include extra women's restrooms, headsets for the hearing impaired, and a variety of concessions scattered around the main and upstairs lobbies. *Tip:* This is haven for those $5 "free" souvenir photographers who often congregate between the concession vendors and the aisle entrances; don't get caught off guard.

The Shows   The Grand Palace has been the Country Music Association's Venue of the Year, and it's a chicken-egg question whether the venue or the stars are responsible for its prominence. Palace partner Kenny Rogers (also in the Silver Dollar City group) plays for a week or so at a time and brings in a full two-hour, two-act production with dancers, back-up band, video and lighting effects, etc., and is reliably variety-series seasoned. Rogers' voice, his multitude of hits, and his personal "Gambler" charm are his signature, and he's clearly the biggest draw; his usual duet partner is the appealingly husky Kim Carnes ("Betty Davis Eyes"). Tickets for Rogers range up to $33 without tax.

The big-name country guest stars, along with some pop attractions—Reba McEntire, Neil Sedaka, Tanya Tucker, John Anderson, Anne Murray—most often come in on "Super Sundays," and ticket prices can go to around $38. The Radio City Christmas Spectacular with the Rockettes runs through the Thanksgiving and Christmas holidays.

Hughes Brothers Celebrity Theatre

Location   Lodge of the Ozarks at 3425 W. Hwy. 76, just west of Gretna

Open   April through mid-December

Show   The World Famous Platters

Type of Show   50s and 60s Motown classics

Showtimes   Monday through Saturday, 2 and 7 p.m.

Ticket Prices   Adults $22; Children 16 and under free

Other Shows on Site   The Hughes Brothers

Showtimes   Monday–Saturday, 9:30 a.m.

Ticket Prices   Adults $19; Children 6–12 $6

Reservations and Information   (800) 422-0076

Dark   Sundays

Seating Capacity   1,200

Disabled Access   Good

Overall Rating   ★★½

General Description   The Celebrity Theatre, an extension of the Lodge of the Ozarks, is a complex of its own, including balcony seating which serves as a dinner theater (much like a racetrack concourse), a down the hall lounge called Club Celebrity, and an adjacent restaurant which serves up culinary counterparts to meal/show packages. Downstage right is a souvenir booth and in the lobby you'll find concessions and a gift shop. The theater is wide with a large center section flanked by two narrow sections that are divided by spacious aisles and two aisles along the walls. The seats are comfortably cushioned-but-worn auditorium-styled seats. Even though the sound system is a cluster of speakers over the front center of the auditorium, the shows here consists of good acoustics without being over-amped. *Tip:* The back third of the theater sits beneath the balcony where a couple of support poles near the aisles obstruct some views. Our choice seating is about one third the way back in the center section.

The Show   The Platters deliver a performance that surpasses many of the nostalgia-riddled shows Branson has to offer. Lawrence Randle, Eddie Stoval, Walter White, and Dee Dee Hamilton have a poignancy in their voices that makes Platter's hits "The Great Pretender," "Harbor Lights," and "Only You" as amazing as the first time you heard them. Don't expect them to do all the performing, though. It is very likely that some bashful audience member will be requested to join the group on stage, enjoy the spotlight and join in a song. The Platters are also supported by The Do-Wop Band, a 5-piece ensemble that plays upstage on a raised platform. The production includes colorful stage lights, several costume changes, and lots of warm feelings. Occasionally, the pace of the performance will be brutally interrupted by emcee Brent Aitchison and his dry impersonation routine. If you can endure Aitchison, then you will be served a most delightful show by the Platters.

The Morning Show   The Hughes Brothers, their wives, parents, and occasionally children and the family dog wake audiences up with a variety show of music, comedy, and dancing. Having recently purchased the Celebrity Theatre, the Hughes Brothers are pleased to find a permanent home in Branson.

Jennifer's Americana Theater

Location   2905 W. Highway 76, a block west of Wildwood Drive

Open   April through mid-December

Type of Show   Celebrity concert

Showtimes   Monday–Saturday, 9:30 a.m., and limited 8 p.m. shows

Ticket Prices $19 adults; children ages 12 and under free

Reservations and Information   (417) 335-3664; www.jennifer.com

Dark   Sundays

Seating Capacity   950

Disabled Access   Fair

Overall Rating   ★★½

General Description   Jennifer's Theater is a fairly straightforward auditorium, with the seats arranged in three sections and two aisles running all the way down. The floor angle is fairly slight, but the stage is elevated, and no views are obstructed by poorly placed poles. The general furnishings are quite plain; and while the seats are generic they are not uncomfortable. The sound and lighting boards are in an open box at the rear of the auditorium. Parking is in the rear; the ticket booth is inside. The concession and gift shops are both modest.

The Show High-energy local Jennifer Wilson is a Branson-style American success story. Working her way up from a chorus singer and dancer, and finally headlining her own show in the early 90s, she has gathered a decent following on the strength of her live performances.

The show includes a live band, dancers, and the obligatory hillbilly comedian. Jennifer sings, taps, clogs, chats up the audience, and changes costumes faster than a speeding bullet. Her band is good and her voice is strong, although it can be a little canned at times, or alternately, a little breathy. Her best known number is "Grandpa," and watching the thirty-something Jennifer fondle the oldest man in the audience while she pleads, "Grandpa, tell me about the way it used to be . . ." could be counted as Branson's best-veiled steamy number.

We find Jennifer's show fast-paced and interesting, but a t times a little forced. Kids probably won't go for it, but older folks, especially older men, enjoy it.

Kirby Van Burch Theatre

Location 470 State Hwy. 248, just west of 65

Open May through mid-December

Type of Show Magic and illusion

Showtimes Tuesday through Sunday, 2 p.m.; Saturday, 8 p.m.

Ticket Prices $25 adults; $15 children ages 3–13; $75 for 2–3 adults and children.

Reservations and Information (417) 337-7140

Dark Mondays

Seating Capacity 2,000

Disabled Access Excellent

Overall Rating ★★★½

General Description Like any magician, Van Burch must feel the overwhelming need to outdo his last trick. Having finished our review for the Kirby Van Burch Theatre we found that he had disappeared from his former location . . . and reappeared not too far away, next door to the Wayne Newton Theater!

The Show A show of illusion and magic of the highest calliber, Kirby Van Burch easily earns his title, "Prince of Magic." Every generation will be wide-eyed as Van Burch morphs his assistants into dangerous animals of the jungle, and the audience remains mesmerized as he levitates inanimate objects across the stage. His sets are simple but flashy with steel plated cages and shiny glass crates within which the illusions occur. The show moves quickly—you won't want to blink. Have you ever wanted to perform magic? Well here you just might as Van Burch has the occasional need for additional assistants—not that anything has ever happened to his other assistants, he just wants you to share in the experience firsthand. At the end of the show you'll find your children riveted to the ends of their seats. *Tip:* The Christmas special might be produced in the best of intentions, however, Van Burch is a magician and not an actor. The fairytale drama languishes on and on as people miss lines and break character in a most amateur fashion. The illusions thrown into the play were nothing to compare to what had already been performed and in fact seems included only as an obligation. Young children in the audience probably won't be so critical because the sets are embellished and the costumes colorful. Adults, bring a good book.

Legends Family Theater

Location   3600 W. Highway 76, west of the Gretna Road/165 intersection

Open   February through December

Type of Show   Production show

Showtimes   Thursday–Tuesday, 2 p.m. and 8 p.m.

Ticket Prices $24 adults; $5 children ages 4 through 16

Reservations and Information   (888) 330-7469

Dark   Wednesdays

Seating Capacity   1,300

Disabled Access   Fair

Overall Rating   ★★

General Description   This is another of the older, high-school-style theaters, with straight-on views, a plain stage, two side aisles, and no obstructions. Although the theater itself is fairly old, the sound system has been powerfully upgraded by the addition of state-of-the-art sound board and speakers (visible at the rear of the auditorium).

The Show   *Legends in Concert* is a musical production show featuring a highly talented cast of impersonators who re-create the stage performances of such celebrities as Elvis, Reba McEntire, Conway Twitty, Hank Williams Jr., the Blues Brothers, and Neil Diamond. Impersonators actually sing and/or play their own instruments , so there's no lip-syncing or faking. In additions to the Branson and Las Vegas productions, *Legends in Concert* also fields a road show. The third show makes possible a continuing exchange of performers between the productions, so that the shows are always changing. In addition to the impersonators, *Legends* features an unusually hot and creative company of dancers, much in the style of TV's Solid Gold Dancers. There are no variety acts.

The show is a barn-burner and possibly, minute-for-minute, the fastest-moving show in town. The impersonations are extremely effective, replicating the physical appearances, costumes, mannerisms, and voices of the celebrities with remarkable likeness. While each show features the work of about eight stars, with a roster that ensures something for patrons of every age, certain celebrities (most notably Elvis) are always included. Regardless of the stars impersonated, *Legends in Concert* is fun, happy, and upbeat. It's a show that establishes rapport with the audience—a show that makes you feel good.

The Wayne Newton Theater

Location   464 Highway 248, just west of 65

Open   May through mid-December

Type of Show   Celebrity headliners

Frequent Headliners   Wayne Newton

Showtimes   Tuesday–Sunday, 8 p.m. (June, October, and November)

Ticket Prices $29 adults; $15 children 12 and under

Other Shows on Site   Acrobats of China

Showtimes   Saturday–Thursday, 3 and 8 p.m.

Ticket Prices $23 adults; $12 children 3 to 18; family pass (2 adults, up to 3 kids) $58

Morning Show   The Lowe Family of Utah

Showtimes   Monday–Thursday and Saturdays, 10 a.m.

Ticket Prices $20 adults; children 12 and under free

Reservations and Information   (417) 335-2000; www.waynenewton.com

Dark   Varies

Seating Capacity   2,200

Disabled Access   Excellent

Overall Rating   No rating available at press time.

General Description   The Talk of the Town Theater is one of the newest, best-equipped, and most comfortable, with wide seats and good leg room. The front entrance to the lobby is mostly glass and wood, a sort of elegant barn style, and the main curtain is among the decorative highlights in town, a great golden-tinged mural of an Ozark hoedown. Two large projection screens on either side of the stage display both pre-produced film and live on-stage video from hand-held minicams, expertly "overlaid" and time-delayed in very Hollywood-pro fashion. Lighting and sound equipment are also new and state of the art. *Tip:* Wheelchair "parking" in the back of the wide transverse aisle may block the first rows of seats right behind; ask for seats in the central area of the left or right section instead. The theater offers fair visibility from even far edges, but the show is "pointed" pretty much ahead. Special features include a large "time-out" room to the rear with a bathroom, changing table, etc.

The Show   Wayne Newton will perform regularly in 2000. His performances are known for quality, and seldom include elaborate productions.

Other Shows   The Acrobats of China are appearing for the first time in Branson in the 2000 season. The New Shanghai Circus claims that "they perform the impossible." These are well-trained acrobats that can do everything from body contorting to magic. Great child as well as adult appeal.

The Morning Show   The Lowe Family of Utah is comprised of Mom, Dad, and seven children, varying in ages from mid-teens to mid-twenties. In the tradition of the Osmonds, this family performs their own brand of a singing and dancing variety show.

The Osmond Family Theatre

Location   3216 W. Hwy. 76, east of the 165/Gretna Rd. intersection

Open   Mid-April through December

Type of Show   Music, comedy, ice skating variety

Show   Osmonds

Showtimes   Monday–Saturday, 2 and 8 p.m. (April through June, and September through December)

Ticket Prices $27.50 adults; children $5

Other Show on Site   Tony Orlando

Showtimes   Monday–Saturday, 2 and 8 p.m. (last two weeks of June and October)

Ticket Prices $28 adults; children 3–12 are free from April through June, and $10, September–December. Also, lunch for all shows is an additional $12 for adults and $6 for children. Dinner is an extra $18 for adults and $8 for children.

Other Show on Site   Flashback, a musical celebration on ice

Showtimes   Monday–Saturday, 8 p.m. (July and August only)

Ticket Prices $19 adults; children 12 and under are free

Early Show   Phillip Wellford

Showtimes   Monday–Saturday, 10 a.m. (July and August, 2 p.m.)

Ticket Prices $20 adults; $5 children ages 6–12

Reservations and Information   (800) 477-6102

Dark   Sundays

Seating Capacity   1,164

Disabled Access   Fair

Overall Rating   ★★★★

General Description   The Osmond Family Theatre is unusually simple and elegant, black with a few Deco touches and "glass" brick risers and lighting effects largely limited to the mirror ball overhead. Visibility throughout is good, thanks to a subtle combination of ramps and risers; the chairs are unusually comfortable, with more lumbar support than most. The ice rink provides an area for back-up visual enhancement during vocal performances and also serves as a mainstage in and of itself.

The Show   This is an unpretentious but professional, fully rehearsed, and fully enjoyable show, one that gets a high rating even from post-pop skeptics. It is family-style entertainment in both senses of the word: Depending on who is in Branson at any given time, anywhere from 4 to 12 Osmonds may entertain, but the original quartet—Merrill, Jay, Alan, and Wayne—plus littlest brother (now musical director and financial whiz) Jimmy are the mainstays. The production is upbeat and reasonably slick, with the usual backup vocalists in sequins. All-ages attraction is fairly high, but guest appearances by the suprisingly dance-hip teenthrobs the "Second Generation Osmonds" (four sons of the sons) will clinch it for the under-16 crowd. The pace is fairly rapid, with change-up magic tricks and some very hammy humor, instrumental variety displays, and even some barbershop harmony along with the requisite patriotic number, which seems more controlled and less pandering than some.

Tony Orlando returns to play the Osmond Family Theater on select dates to perform his popular hit songs, including "Tie a Yellow Ribbon Round the Ole' Oak Tree." All shows feature the skating talents of the Ice Angels, the amusing comedy of Jim Barber and Friends, vocalist Babette Young, and the Jay Osmond Band.

The Other Show   "Flashback" is an ice skating variety show, featuring a musical journey from the 1950s to the present day.

The Early Show   Wake up laughing with the juggling-savvy and slapstick comedy of Phillip Wellford wrapped up in a bright, banana-colored, 40s-style zoot suit. You might want to point to your old physics textbook and exclaim that some objects weren't meant to fly, but don't tell that to Wellford! If it isn't permanently affixed to the ground you're sure to see it juggled. His slapstick and repartee may seem forced at times but his talent is genuine.

The morning show is accompanied by the jive/swing band Five Guys Named Moe , that plays several short sessions while Wellford prepares for more waggish mayhem. Susan, his wife, participates as the quick-quipped assistant for Wellford and backup vocalist for the band. Patty Davidson, the only rough spot in the line-up, adds a sluggishly paced ventriloquism act to Wellford's otherwise entertaining show. *Tip:* Folks planning on breakfast before the show should allow enough time to digest their hearty morning meal.

Owens Theater

Location   205 S. Commercial in downtown Branson

Open   February through December

Type of show   Elvis impersonation and musical revue spoof

Showtimes   Friday–Tuesday, 8 p.m.; Friday and Tuesday, 3 p.m.

Ticket Prices $20 adults; $5 children ages 6–16; VIP seats add $5 per ticket

Reservations and Information   (417) 336-2112 or (800) ELVIS-95; www.elvisbranson.com

Dark   Wednesdays and Thursdays

Seating Capacity   225

Disabled Access   Good

Overall Rating   ★★★

General Description   The Owens is the oldest theater in Branson and its modest and aging interior and exterior are evidence of that. It opened in 1935—the year Elvis was born. The Owens is at the opposite end of the spectrum from the Grand Palace, and yet the building has its own power as an artifact with a comfortable familiarity that can't be built, but can be built upon. The seats are old, but not uncomfortable, and the two aisles are wide enough to give the small, deep house an open feeling. The stage is a mere fifteen feet from the front row. Lighting and technical equipment is brand-new and state of the art. Wheelchairs will have an easy time rolling into the small lobby/gift shop and then ramp gently on into the theater.

The Show "Elvis and the Superstars" is a one-of-a-kind venue in Branson, and for those who love "The King" or who have a good sense of musical kitsch, the show is not to be missed. Starring Dave "Elvis" Ehlert, who has been impersonating Elvis for 30 years, the show is a one-man tour-de-force. Dave really sings Elvis's hits well, and his dancing and stage presence are very convincing. The first half is pure Elvis in all his many moods, and the second half is a whirlwind spoof with Ehlert "becoming" Roy Orbison, Willie Nelson, Stevie Wonder, Liberace, Neil Diamond, Johnny Mathis, Julio Iglesias, Tom Jones, and others! Various performers make appearances as The Blues Brothers, Ann Margaret, and there's a surprise visit from a different "king." "Elvis and the Superstars" may be too camp for some, but the Elvis impersonation is a genuine piece of work deserving praise. The "get up on your hind legs, go out there and entertain 'em" factor makes this a standout in Branson. For something completely different, don't miss it.

Tip: The show goes on the road for two weeks during the middle of April and also during the end of October.

The Presleys' Country Jubilee Theater

Location   2920 W. Highway 76, a block west of the Grand Palace

Open   March through mid-December

Type of Show   Music-comedy variety

Showtimes   Monday–Saturday, 8 p.m. (warm-up show 7:30)

Ticket Prices $20 adults; $10 children ages 4–12; ages 3 and under free; $54.50 family pass for 2 adults and up to 5 children under age 18

Reservations and Information   (417) 334-4874; www.presleys.com

Dark   Sundays

Seating Capacity   2,000

Disabled Access   Good

Overall Rating   ★★½

General Description   The theater looks from the outside like one of the original barns, but inside it's pretty straightforward: typical chairs, two long aisles down to the stage that split the seating in thirds, and a small balcony. Rear seats beneath the balcony are not obstructed, but may miss a few of the lighting effects. Lighting is old-show spots, overhead and from the balcony. The stage itself is very plain, just an elevated rectangle.

The Show   This is one of the original Branson shows, and it adheres to the old formula: a little country, a little fiddling, some boots, some sequins, some very broad comedy, and a family atmosphere. It's still a family operation, and among the most famous characters in Bransonia is Gary Presley's ultra-Ozarkian "Herkimer." Other longtimers include Steve Presley, a drummer who looks like a cross between a Revolutionary War casualty and Yosemite Sam; general granddaddy Lloyd, and an Osmond-like third generation of younger entertainers. The family is backed by a full band and singers, dancers, etc. This show will seem very simple to TV regulars, but has an old and honorable history, and lives up to its perceived "role" as the Strip's oldest show. All ages do pretty well here: the warm-up comedy show, featuring "Harley and Rick," is particularly easy for kids to understand.

The Promise Theater

Location   755 Gretna Road at Wildwood Drive

Open   April through mid-December

Type of Show   Spiritual theatrical production

Show   *The Promise*

Showtimes   Monday–Saturday, 8 p.m.

Ticket Prices $28 adult; $15 children ages 7–12; ages 6 and under free; $15 pastor

Other Shows on Site   *Two From Galilee*

Showtimes   Monday–Saturday, 3 p.m. (November and December only)

Ticket Prices $28 adult; $15 children ages 7–12; ages 6 and under free; $15 pastor

Reservations and Information   (417) 336-4202

Dark   Sundays

Seating Capacity   2,000

Disabled Access   Excellent

Overall Rating   ★★★★

General Description   This is one of the newest venues, and shows it—a big, arching glass and sandstone auditorium in the modern-Opry style that the Wayne Newton Theater also nods to. The lobby is spare and airy, brick- and sandstone-colored.

The interior space is wide, with total visibility (though sitting at the sides may be a little tiring on the neck) and first-rate acoustics—volume balance panels overhead and built-in house mics. The sound board is extremely expensive and up-to-date. The rest of the money may be in the chairs—firm and comfortable, with extremely soft cushions but good lumbar support, a little extra elbow room, and a lot of extra leg room—they may offer the best seating in town. *Tip:* A wide aisle runs parallel to the stage about halfway back, and although the front row of seats immediately behind that aisle may seem desirable, it is actually the only row not canted above the row in front, because it's set on the aisle level to accommodate disabled folks in wheelchairs. It's fair to expect that your view may be slightly blocked by the parked wheelchairs should you sit in this row.

The Show   *The Promise* was Branson's 1997, 1998, and 1999 Show of the Year. Combining the life of Christ; more than 50 singing performers; special effects including smoke, lasers, and a rain curtain; flying angels; and several species of live animals; this comes as no surprise. Wrapped in an "Our Town" contemporary narrator's story of his renewed love for Jesus, *The Promise* is a can't miss hit for folks who like their Christianity spelled out on stage. The interpretation here is quite literal and quite severe at one point with much agonizing, quivering, and jerking on the cross that may be too intense for young children. 1997, 1998, and 1999 Male Vocalist of the Year, Randy Brooks, plays Jesus. A long production with a running time of 2 hours 20 minutes, the comfort of the seats is a true Godsend. Find out more at the web site: www.thepromise.com. Here you can also purchase a video, audiotape, or CD; make reservations; and download video.

Other Shows   *Two From Galilee* is the story of Mary and Joseph before the birth of Jesus. Touted as the newest muscial experience in Branson and one that will have you both laughing and crying, this proves to be a great second effort from the same producers and much of the cast of *The Promise.*

Ronnie Prophet Pickin' Parlor Theatre

Location   Shepherd of the Hills Homestead

Open   Late April through mid-December

Type of Show   Country

Showtimes   Monday–Saturday, 9:30 a.m.

Ticket Prices $15 adults; children 16 and under free with adult

Reservations and Information   (800) 653-6288; www.oldmatt.com

Dark   Sundays

Seating Capacity   150

Disabled Access   Fair

Overall Rating   ★★★

General Description   The Ronnie Prophet Pickin' Parlor Theatre is part of the Shepherd of the Hills Homestead (see page 119). Like the rest of the property, this showroom is simple and unassuming with rough-cut timber walls and is adorned with memorabilia of country music and country life. There are no worries of being lost in the restrooms here. That is to say, you won't find any hand-carved billiards tables. In the theater, seating consists of conference room–styled chairs with cushioned backs and seats. These can be rearranged to accommodate any special seating needs. Although the sound and light systems are rudimentary, they make the most of them. In truth, the size of this facility does not require more juice than the systems offer. *Tip:* It can be quite a walk from the remote parking lot to the theater—don't arrive late.

The Show   Ronnie Prophet is no stranger to country music. With a multitude of albums, chart records, and television show appearances, Ronnie Prophet has entertained country music fans for years. A native of Canada and former resident of Nashville, in Branson you will find he has relaxed into this quaint and intimate theater where audiences will revel in his magnificent guitar playing. I was personally overwhelmed as Prophet played "Yankee Doodle" on his guitar with one hand while blending it with "Dixie" using his other.

Prophet will also bring a smile to your face, not with far fetched comic antics (okay, there were these masks . . .), but with impressions of your favorite old-school country musicians like Chet Atkins, Johnny Cash, and Hank Williams, Sr., as well as a few he has the audience suggest. Ronnie Prophet doesn't perform alone. He is joined by his wife, Glory-Anne Prophet, a splendid country music vocalist in her own right, with records and awards to compare with his. Glory-Anne is an essential part of this show, adding her charm and humor to that of Ronnie's. Ray Wix accompanies Prophet on many songs, enriching the sound. Also, like other shows in Branson, Prophet's show does have a comic relief. But unlike many of those other shows, Dotty Booth's character, "Bessie Bug," does not disrupt the show. Instead, she wanders playfully in and out of the show from time to time to stir up some trouble or a laugh. By far this is one of the most sincere and personable shows Branson offers. *Tip:* Ronnie Prophet and cast put on a must-see. Leave the barrage of Branson traffic and signage behind and don't miss this show!

The Remington Theater

Location   3701 W. Hwy. 76, just east of Shepherd of the Hills Expressway intersection

Open   Mid-February through December

Show   *Cirque Lumiere: Imagination Triumphant*

Type of Show   Illusion, comedy, and acrobatic variety show

Showtimes   Monday–Saturday, 3 and 7:30 p.m. (May through December)

Ticket Prices $29 adults; $17 children ages 6–17

Other Shows on Site   Magic of the Night

Showtimes   Monday–Saturday, 7 p.m. (February through April only)

Ticket Prices $22 adults; $13 children ages 6–17

Reservations and Information   (417) 336-6220; www.remingtontheater.com

Dark   Sundays

Seating Capacity   2,700

Disabled Access   Very good

Overall Rating   No rating available since these are brand-new shows for 2000

General Description   This is one of Branson's most "fantastic" buildings. Ozark businessman Jim Thomas opened the theater in the early 90s as The Five Star Theater, and leased it to Van Burch and Wellford, and then to Wayne Newton. From 1997–99, the theater was home to the award-winning Branson City Lights/All Star Revue show. In building on that tradition of excellence in entertainment, *Cirque Lumiere* combines the best elements of the Branson City Lights show with dazzling new scenes. To prepare the theater for the arrival of Cirque, a new state-of-the-art lighting and special effects system has been installed, together with revolutionary changes in sound and staging capabilities. Other changes in seating, food concessions, and theater operations have also been completed.

The Show   *Cirque Lumiere,* created by Gary Ouellet, features the best illusionists, comedians, jugglers, ice skaters, acrobats and dancers from all over the world. The Hamners, the talented husband-and-wife team, will be performing a death-defying illusion "Vertigo" as well as "Stargate," "Origami," "The New Metamorphosis," and other one-of-a-kind feats. According to theater manager Andrew Marsh, "It is a circus of light, but also a carnival of sound, a festival of motion, and a visual flight of imagination and fantasy that will bring audiences right up out of their seats."

Other Shows   For the year 2000's Hot Winter Fun season, the Remington will be hosting *Magic of the Night* for a limited time. The same two Hamners that will be part of *Cirque Lumiere* host two hours of breathtakingly amazing feats—plus music, dance, and other top variety acts.

76 Music Hall

Location   1945 W. Hwy. 76, between Forsythe Street and Truman Road

Open   Mid-January through mid-December

Type of Show   Revue venue; multiple shows

Showtimes   Sunday, 2 p.m. and 7 p.m.; Monday–Saturday, 10 a.m.,
 1, 3:30, and 8 p.m.

Ticket Prices $19.50 adult; children ages 12 and under free

Reservations and Information   (417) 335-2484

Seating Capacity   550

Disabled Access   Good

Overall Rating   ★★½

General Description   The actual auditorium suggests that it started out as
the movie house at the far end of an old shopping mall—either that, or a
school auditorium. The stage is high off the ground, square and quite
plain; the seats are standard old-cinema issue: metal backs and arms, fold-
ing red cushion, minimal leg room. There are also some obstructed views
from big pillars, but the room is small, so rear-row seats are no problem.

The Shows   The individual programs vary in style and appeal, and many
of the same performers double up during the day.

The Headline Show   *76 Country USA* is a fast-paced country music variety
show which includes the usual spattering of gospel, and of course, the goofy
country clown and sequined "girl singer." The polished band includes Doug
Huffman, the former drummer of the rock band Boston, so it may be one
of the biggest thirty-something draws in Branson. And the show's vocal
quartet, Pierce Arrow, is notable for its freakish bass singer who holds the
Guinness Book of World Records record for singing the lowest note ever
recorded. Although his technical skills are pretty amazing, most people
would rather hear the notes than feel them. The comedian in this show is
a seasoned Branson performer whose act is a about as bawdy as Branson
gets. The show doesn't offer much to teens and children, but adults of all
ages will enjoy it.
 Reality check: Lights and props are minimal, and the sound system is
really not equipped to deal with the mega-bass singer from the quartet, but
the show is sincere and intimate with a fun cast and few gimmicks.

Other Shows   Mornings bring *The Brumley Music Show,* an Ozark-style
music review, while early afternoons bring the *Down Home Country Show,*
and Sunday afternoons bring the *Sunday Gospel Show.*
 Tip: The 76 Complex has actually expanded into two malls side by side;
the theater mall also houses a 3-D cinema, indoor miniature golf course, and
video arcade; the addition has several shops and restaurants—plus a 320-
room inn with spa and pools. This makes it a premiere rainy-day destination.

The Showboat *Branson Belle*

Location   4800 Highway 165, just south of Table Rock Dam

Open   April through December

Type of Show   Dining music variety show

Headline Show   *Steppin' Out*

Showtimes   Monday–Saturday, 8 a.m., 11 a.m., 4:30 p.m., and 8 p.m.; Sunday showtimes vary.

Ticket Prices   Breakfast: $27 adults; $10 children ages 12 and under. Lunch: $30 adults; $13 children ages 12 and under. Dinner: $36 adults; $15 children ages 12 and under

Reservations and Information   (800) 227-8587

Seating Capacity   700

Disabled Access   Poor

Overall Rating   ★★★

General Description   The Showboat *Branson Belle* slipped into Table Rock Lake in the mid-90s along two tracks lubricated with banana peels. Since then it has cruised the lake offering surprisingly palatable meals along with entertainment.

We include the *Branson Belle* with theaters because the shows usually last almost the entire duration of the cruise, leaving no time to step out on deck and enjoy the scenery. (It makes you wonder why you ever left the dock.)

The interior of the showboat is in keeping with its Mississippi River boat theme, and includes tightly packed banks of tables situated on a main level and balcony. Windows are few, and placed in such a manner that it is impossible to view outdoor scenery.

Tip: Restrooms (especially women's) are few and far between. Keep this in mind if you're planning to wait until the show is over. Also, realize that gratuity for your server is not included in the price of the dinner. As a whole, the staff is excellent, and we suggest $3 per person as tip.

The Show   "Steppin' Out Into the New Milennium" is a musical journey through the most memorable songs of the past 100 years, hosted by the talented Steve Grimm and the Steppin' Out Orchestra. In addition, the Russian duo of Andrei and Marina present an incredibly graceful and almost unbelievable acrobatic dance performance. And to top it all off, there's Todd Oliver and Irving, the talking dog. We laughed until we cried, our noses ran and lying in the floor became necessary. By far the best ventriloquist in Branson. *Tips:* Many tables run perpendicular to the stage, forcing you to crane your neck to view the show. Request a table which runs parallel to the stage and at least 20 feet away so that you sit facing the stage. Wheelchair-restricted folks should arrive at least 30 minutes ahead of time to comfortably descend the ramps leading to the boat.

Yakov Smirnoff's What a Country Theater

Location   3750 W. Highway 76, just east of Shepherd of the Hills Expressway

Open   April through mid-December

Show   *Yakoff Smirnov Show*

Type of Show   Comedy production

Showtimes   Monday–Saturday, 9 a.m. and 3 p.m.

Ticket Prices $25 adults; children ages 11 and under free

Reservations and Information   (417) 336-6547 or (800) 33-NOKGB; www.yakov.com

Dark   Sundays

Seating Capacity   1,350

Disabled Access   Good

Overall Rating   ★★★

General Description   A huge complex, the building is reminiscent of St. Peter's Basilica meets Long Island kitsch. The mostly white exterior is trimmed with red and blue, and colonnades flank a grand entrance. Yakov's What A Country Theater is an upscale version of the 76 Mall, in that it contains a restaurant, shops, and two theaters; the What a World Show-club houses nearly continuous rotating acts from around the world, while the What a Country Theater houses the headline show. The international theme is carried through at the restaurant, which offers various ethnic cuisines (nothing too wild, mind you) and servers dressed in costumes of various cultures. Shops contain gifts from all over the world, and artisans demonstrate craft-making from various cultures.

The Show   Former Russian comic Yakov Smirnoff is quite funny on the subject of coming to grips with American society, slang, advertising, and superstition: his increasing collection of video clips featuring his wife and small children are centerpieces of the act. He plays the patriotic number, too, but with more irony (and more reason than most); being sworn in as a citizen is the high point of his life, and the very next minute, he echoes, "I hate those foreigners—they take our jobs!" It gets a big laugh. It also makes you suspect that the fire-engine red Ferrari in the parking lot is a bit of living well and best revenge.

The Jim Stafford Theater

Location   3440 W. Highway 76, between Gretna Drive and Shepherd of the Hills Expressway

Open   February through December

Type of Show   Music-comedy variety

Showtimes   Daily, 8 p.m.

Ticket Prices $28 adults; $8.50 children ages 7–12; ages 6 and under free

Reservations and Information   (417) 335-8080; www.jimstafford.com

Seating Capacity   1,120

Disabled Access   Good

Overall Rating   ★★★½

General Description   Whoever has the franchise for painting faux marble in Branson must have struck it rich: Stafford's lobby columns and walls are lavished with emerald green (snake green?) marbling. The lobby is relatively small because of the semi-grand staircase up to the cafe; the gift shop is around the corner to the right, and ticket booths to the side. The parking lot around back is a little steep, but there is a let-off or walkup area in front. Inside, the red wall fabric is gathered into marquis-like "stones"—a subtle echo of the spider-web lighting that recalls his hit "Spiders and Snakes"—and there is old-style gold swagging around. *Clustering hint:* Stafford's theater is in a tight cluster with the Celebrity, Moe Bandy, Mickey Gilley, and the Duttons.

A small number of wheelchair spaces are down front, and ambulatory relatives may sit right behind them. View lines are all fine in this modestly sized room; sound and lighting, good. There's a "changing room" in back, and the sound booth is elevated, so there is no obstruction.

The Show   This show has very high family appeal for all ages—perhaps the highest kids' rating of any major musical performance. After all, Stafford, who is both energetic and endearing, bills himself as Branson's "biggest kid at heart." (You might think that at less than a year old, Stafford's daughter was too young to make it onto the Family Values list, but you'd be wrong; doting papa Stafford had her up for a few minutes.) Son Sheaffer, at the ripe old age of five, is now a permanent addition to the variety of the show. If his fiddle number doesn't make your heart smile, wait 'til you see him behind that shiny red drum set! Balloons, blimps, toys, stupid pet tricks, you name it, "Mr. Spiders and Snakes" is willing to try it. Anyone willing to wear those plaid jackets has no shame, anyway. And his band is similarly free-spirited, lending an almost vaudeville tone to the proceedings.

Note that Stafford is one of the "Branson Year-rounders," those performers who've decided to stay open during the winter except for a short break at the first of the year. January and February shows are Thursday –Saturday at 8 p.m. and Sunday at 2 p.m. Also, although Stafford regularly performs at 2 only on Sundays, he adds other matinees during various times of the year and compensates by going dark on Mondays in February, April, and May. Ask specifically about desired dates.

Added attraction: In addition to the ordinary concession stand, the theater also holds a cafe, called "Pie-Annie's," that serves lunch and dinner; but there is no direct view of the show and no package rate except for tour groups. For more information see "Restaurants and Dining."

Starlite Theatre

Location 3115 W. Hwy. 76

Open April through December; February and March, call for schedule

Show Lost in the Fifties

Type of Show Musical review

Showtimes 2 and 8 p.m.

Ticket Prices Adults $26.50; children 12 and under $6.50

Other Shows on Site Doug Gabriel, *The Starlite Kids Review*

Showtimes Doug Gabriel, 9:30 a.m.; Starlite Kids, 5:30 p.m.

Ticket Prices Doug Gabriel: adults $21; children 16 and under free; *Starlite Kids:* adults $20; children 12 and under $6.50

Reservations and Information (887)336-STAR

Dark *Fifties* and *Starlite Kids,* Fridays; Doug Gabriel, varies

Seating Capacity 880

Disabled Access Good

Overall Rating ★★½

General Description Entering the all-glass enclosed atrium of the Starlite Theatre takes you back to life in the 1950s, complete with the strolling lane, park benches, and real trees. Tickets are purchased underneath the marquis, located between the snack bar and the gift shop. In this beautiful new venue you will find somewhat unexpected amenities; very comfortable seating, vast leg room, even cup holders for your sodas. Theoretically, one could spend all day at the Starlite, with three different shows offered at staggered times and a true fifties-style diner to satiate your craving for a butterscotch malt between performances (see Restaurants and Dining for a detailed review). When ordering tickets, request at least 15 rows back from the stage. Due to the "production" of the shows, any closer will not allow you to see the performance in the big picture. Plus, the lighting and sound are of such high quality that they are more appreciated the further back you are.

The stage is elevated for a great view even from the back row, and the high-tech production booth is tucked into the back wall, as not to obstruct or distract. *Tip:* Wheelchair seating is located all the way to the front on the very ends of the left and right sections next to the walls (basically, the worst seats in the house).

The Show   Lost in the Fifties is a high-energy, fast-paced show, complete with bobby socks, white T-shirts, vintage vehicles, and an impressive Elvis impersonator. The performers are very polished, both in their singing and dancing. Everything is enhanced a degree by the stunning production of the show. Lights, sound, props, costumes and sets are of the latest technological quality. The problem with the show, ironically, also lies in the production. It's like a television commercial. At times, you have to stop and wonder if you are trying to be sold something. The intent is to "transport" the viewer back to those familiar times; instead, the performers act like actors. There is a point in the show where clips of songs are so short that it sounds like the latest Time/Life boxed set advertisement. The show comes off as a bunch of kids trying to act like they fit within an age that they know nothing about.

Other Shows   The Starlite Kids Review is a terrific show to take your own aspiring youngsters to go see. The Starlite Kids appeal to all ages. The talent of most of these children is astounding. Even when the occasional off-key note comes through, it is sung out with innocent, warm happiness. We found the performances to be a bit reminiscent of early *Star Search* episodes, with the belting voices, glittery costumes, and beaming parents (you can always pick them out in the crowd . . .) The show was a bit too loud, but not distractingly so.

Doug Gabriel Show: With a good voice, quick guitar, and a friendly personality, Doug Gabriel takes you on a musical tour from tributes to country-western stars like Roy Clark and Chet Atkins to lounge-i-fied interpretations of artists like Elvis and Kenny Rogers or show tunes like "Memories" from *Cats*. Gabriel also interjects some of his originals from time to time. And that is the problem. What Gabriel considers a diverse repertoire, we feel is a loss of focus by trying to be too many things to too many people. He is supported by a 7-piece band that seems to under-perform at times. In addition to the band, Gabriel's wife, Cheryl, his children, and other feature performers participate as well.

The Shoji Tabuchi Theatre

Location   3260 Shepherd of the Hills Expressway, about half a mile east of 76

Open   Mid-March through mid-December

Type of Show   Musical variety

Showtimes   Monday–Saturday, 3 and 8 p.m.

Ticket Price   (with taxes) $29 adults; $28 seniors; $20 children ages 5–12; ages 4 and under in parent's lap free; season pass $160 for all ages

Reservations and Information   (417) 334-7469; www.shoji.com

Dark   Sundays

Seating Capacity   2,000

Disabled Access   Excellent

Overall Rating   ★★★½

General Description   The Tabuchi Theatre is unmistakable, a great purple and silver combination of rococo cinema and Taj Mahal, with marquee lights and poster windows. The lobby is also the most extraordinary in town, and the purple and green women's bathroom—made to resemble a New Orleans conservatory, complete with ferns, fountain, plastic cherubim, and "tin" ceiling—is a tourist attraction in its own right. The men's room is Victorian and has a hand-carved pool table with two rows of chairs for the playing line and a classic chalkboard for scoring. Despite the warning signs, the staff has to be on constant alert to keep would-be sightseers of the wrong sex out of the bathrooms.

As is immediately obvious, Tabuchi's strongest suit (depending on your opinion of his fiddling) is his and his wife and show manager/producer Dorothy's business acumen. There are a half-dozen souvenir booths scattered both upstairs and downstairs. A couple at stage left and right (marked with flashing marquee lights) operate only during intermission. The major gift shops are like a Goldilocks joke, and unabashedly gender stereotypical: Daddy Bear's shop sells fishing equipment and fiddles; Mama Dorothy's is jam-packed with sequined and embroidered clothing, feminine knick-knackery, art glass, and heavy doses of potpourri. Even the gift shops follow the color pattern: his is dark green, hers violet, and Baby Bear's, daughter Christina's shop, is primarily pink. *Tip:* The bathrooms, lobby and shops are all heavily scented—the women's room allegedly orders 80,000 violets, a month—so the allergic should be prepared.

However, the interior of the theater itself is just as carefully constructed, though more subtly. It's full of trap doors and "up periscope" style microphones, flying backdrops, Vegas-clever sets (grand pianos that burst open to reveal a whole cast of dancers), flash pans, etc. The sound system is good, and visuals are uniformly good—no view is obstructed, and all numbers are produced to have 180-degree interest.

The Show   Tickets to the Shoji Tabuchi Theatre are the hottest in town, and with reason. It is by far the most elaborate production, with emphatic laser-light effects (starting with the ones that draw a fiddle and bow playing in the air), "flying" dancers, magic carpets, and fog machines. His audiences are more mixed than most, too, though they are also very heavy on the tour-bus crowd; his sometimes exaggerated foreign-ness seems very attractive to otherwise all-American seniors. Tabuchi is a first-rate audience-worker—a local joke calls Missouri the "Sho-Ji State"—and he and members of the performance come down to chat and sign autographs during the intermission.

A Suzuki-trained musician who "saw the light" at a Roy Acuff show, Tabuchi is a pretty good violinist and a first-class fiddler, but his real forte is his personality: his humor, which must be rehearsed (there are a fair number of jokes about sushi, etc.), is contagious enough that his 18-piece orchestra—possibly the best ensemble in town—clearly enjoys him and the show. They also reportedly rehearse two hours a day, plus six hours' performing, which says a lot about the musical standards.

Family values here, in addition to the flag-waving, are threefold: Tabuchi's face and fiddling, Dorothy's production savvy, and junior star, daughter Christina, who's been on stage since age six—Branson's combination Debby Boone and Shirley Temple—and the attraction around whom the *Aladdin*-style production was developed. She's become a talented young woman, and at age 19, now finds herself singing and dancing as a featured performer.

Tabuchi's shows stand out because of their trained dancers and singers, elaborate costuming, unusually—for Branson—wacky humor and first-class stage sets, notably a malt-shop counter that reverses to a Wurlitzer juke box and stacked-45 dance platforms. He also runs through virtually the entire spectrum of music, including jazz, big band, bluegrass, Latino, pop, classical, Broadway, Disney, gospel, and the heaviest patriotic/religious climax in town, guaranteed to bring the audience to its feet.

Note: Tabuchi presents special Christmas shows which include Sunday night shows; ask about specific date availabilities.

The Mel Tillis Theater

Location   2327 Highway 248, just north of Shepherd of the Hills Expressway

Open   Mid-April through mid-December

Type of Show   Music concert

Showtimes   Tuesday–Sunday, 2 and 8 p.m.

Ticket Prices $31 adults; $15 children ages 4–12; ages 3 and under in parent's lap free

Reservations and Information   (417) 335-6635; www.meltillis.com

Dark   Mondays

Seating Capacity   2,700

Disabled Access   Excellent

Overall Rating   ★★★½

General Description   Mel Tillis's brand new complex, built (like the Grand Palace) to be television ready and with a full recording studio alongside, is vast and imposing, all right—maybe a little too vast. Like most of the artists performing for older audiences, he has chosen to put all his seats on a single floor and tried not to let the rows extend so far back that patrons feel they're in a different room; but with 2,700 seats almost straight across, it loses something in intimacy. And since the theater seems to radiate the same reserved simplicity as Tillis himself, it feels more as if you're in solemn convocation (until the show starts, that is). The angle is not too steep for easy walking; wheelchair parking is along the transverse aisle. No seats are obscured, but although Tillis is aware of the sweep of his room and does remember to move from side to side, seats along the far edges miss some of the effect. The seats are extremely comfortable with maximum leg room.

The stage itself is quite pretty, painted in a opalescent silvery blue-green that resembles abalone-shell jewelry, with a "buckle" over the center that's a nice western-clothing pun. The full-size band—Tillis's longtime Statesiders and a few more—work from big-band style, smoke gray bandstand seats with more of that opalescent trim. A tier of steps, which moves forward to stage front and back, is Tillis's platform. The lighting is proficient rather than flashy, and the acoustics, not surprisingly, are excellent. Behind the doors that lead out from the seats are a second set of doors designed to prevent surges of light (although the ever-vigilant attendants jump to point flashlights at your feet). TV ready, indeed.

The lobby resembles that of a hotel, except for the concession stands. *Tip*: The gift shop is quite large, with clothing, jewelry, souvenirs, miniature license plates and such, and the complete works of Tillis.

The Show   Tillis is not a "showman" in the broad sense, although his decades of self-targeting humor have ironically made his stutter one of country music's signatures (his phone number, we point out, spells 335-M-MEL); and he doesn't make the mistake of playing away from his strengths.

He sings his hits (and there are plenty of them), reminds the audience to buy his records (all available in the lobby and some right down front at the intermission), and leaves the change-up entertainment to whichever off-spring that happen to need launching from the nest at the time. He's in good voice, looks strong, and stands tall; the band is extremely polished. The whole show is pretty straightforward, and may strike a few people as a letdown after the theatrics of, say, Shoji Tabuchi or the energy level at Andy Williams. On the other hand, if you own every one of Tillis's albums, you might well consider this a four-star show. *Family values:* Daughter Pam performs with Tillis frequently throughout the season.

The Bobby Vinton Blue Velvet Theatre

Location   2701 W. Hwy. 76 at Wildwood, across from the Grand Palace

Open   April through mid-December

Type of Show   Musical variety concert

Showtimes   Tuesday–Sunday, 3 and 8 p.m.

Ticket Prices $24 adults; $10 children ages 12 and under

Reservations and Information   (417) 334-2500 or (800) US-BOBBY; www.bobbyvinton.com

Dark   Mondays

Seating Capacity   1,600

Disabled Access   Good

Overall Rating   ★★½

General Description   Bobby Vinton's Blue Velvet Theatre takes blue about as far as it can go: blue "marbled" chairs and floor tiles, blue carpeting with gold "BV" records. What's not blue is bucolic, faux murals on the ceiling like fractured Fragonards and countrysides painted on the bathroom walls (both by "the Italian artist Antonio," who must have graduated from the Famous Artists School). The sight lines are good, and the leg room is good, but the climb up the parking lot is steep enough that Vinton regularly jokes about it. Even the tour buses sometimes have a tough time, but once in, you're okay.

The Show   Vinton is beginning to resemble a Billy Crystal impersonation of himself, but he works hard. He advertises the show as unstructured, and it is at least loose in manner. Like Mel Tillis, Vinton sticks to his own hits, and why not? Every song in the show, as Vinton repeatedly points out, was a gold-record hit, either his or, in the case of "Chattanooga Choo Choo," the Glenn Miller Band's. The rare exceptions include a big-bang salute and a medley from *Phantom of the Opera*. There's a little Polish joking, a little sax-playing, a little soft-shoeing. However, the effect of his obvious hard work—so much perspiring, emoting, etc.—occasionally backfires, and he seems to be paddling hard to keep up with himself. And sometimes, the I'm-as-young-as-ever act makes some of his older fans feel uncomfortable. There is definitely no kids' interest here.

Video screens on either side of the stage bring the Vinton image up close and personal. He also makes himself accessible, kissing women who bring him red roses, in memory of his first hit, "Roses Are Red"—and in fact, if you're late to the show and miss that signature number, he's likely to do an encore on the spot. *Tip:* Vinton occasionally takes a few spins with ladies from the audience, so if you're eager for the chance, or for a smooch, sit in the first 10 or 15 rows along the aisles on either side. Also, couples prepared to dance may be invited up in front of the bandstand; be within waving view. But for better dance opportunities, see the Lawrence Welk listing below.

The Miller Orchestra here is one of three or four such bands sanctioned by the Miller estate, but there are no original members in this rather young ensemble, although one guy played for an early "reconstructed" Miller band and a sax player worked for Guy Lombardo.

The Lawrence Welk Champagne Theatre

Location   1984 Highway 165, about two and a half miles south of 76

Open   April through mid-December

Type of Show   Musical variety

Showtimes   Monday–Saturday, 2 and 8 p.m.

Ticket Prices $29 adults; $10 children ages 6–12; ages 5 and under free; $34 with lunch; $40 with dinner

Other Shows on Site   *The Lennon Brothers' Breakfast Show*

Showtimes   Monday–Saturday, 9:30 a.m.

Ticket Prices $19 adults; $5 children ages 6–12; ages 5 and under free; $24 with breakfast

Reservations and Information   (417) 334-5508; www.welkresort.com

Dark   Sundays

Seating Capacity   Champagne Theatre 2,300

Disabled Access   Excellent

Overall Rating   ★★★½

General Description   The Champagne Theatre/Stage Door Canteen complex is just one of the buildings at the Welk Resort Center, which also includes a fairly luxurious hotel and ultimately will have a second theater, probably with a ballroom, and time-share condos. The building has an old

Silver Screen–era feel, with gold-dusted ticket cages in the center of the lobby and uniformed concessionaires. Good wide aisles and accessible bathrooms. Staff friendliness is very high. The gift shop stocks the full line of Welk videos and records, of course.

The Champagne Theatre itself is a large-scale recreation of the television set—as is the show—complete with huge "window" frames suggesting a baronial veranda, chiffon curtains, chandeliers, and formal bandstand. Despite the large number of seats, visibility is excellent. Seats are a B+, solid and comfortable with slightly nubby upholstery. Wheelchair seating is along the transverse aisle; avoid the seats in the front row of the second tier. The Stage Door Canteen, the restaurant/nightclub at the other end of the lobby, serves a good and varied buffet with a real wine list, appropriately including champagne. (See more under restaurant listings.) *Special features:* Dancing to Welk videos in the Champagne Theatre for an hour before showtime; evening entertainment in the Canteen with the Moonglows.

Tips: Particular fans of Jo Ann Castle should sit to the left, so they can see her play; her piano is set up on the left as you face the stage. In this theater, the very front few rows may be too close; the stage is fairly high, and you may not be able to see the dancing feet.

The Show   Although the man is gone, his champagne hour lives on in reruns: *The Lawrence Welk Show* is PBS's number one syndicated offering, shown on nearly 275 stations. That in itself would probably guarantee good crowds here, since many original cast members and musicians, including the Lennon Sisters, Castle-at-the-piano, and a rotating lineup of other veterans, including vocalist Joe Feening and the rubber-faced, vibes-playing dancer, play here in the (only slightly softer) flesh. In fact, this is a first-class production, fresh, buoyant and accomplished, one of Branson's best bargains even for non-dancers. (For dancers, it's a must—there's almost nowhere else to dance, period.) The veteran and relaxed LW orchestra makes the version of the Glenn Miller Orchestra at Vinton's Blue Velvet, which admittedly plays much less of a role, look sort of wistful; in fact, the first-chair reedman for Miller plays for the Lennon Brothers' morning show.

The Morning Show   Speaking of which, the Lennon Brothers (actually, three Brothers and one sister-in-law) also produce the must-see breakfast show, a lively and warm recreation of Canteen hits from the 30s and 40s, plus a few from the 50s. Admission includes an all-you-can-eat breakfast from an unusually attractive buffet. After breakfast, guests are ushered into the Champagne Theatre for the show.

Tip: The breakfast show is listed as starting at 9:30, but breakfast actually starts at 8; get there in time to get served and have your plates cleared before showtime. And incidentally, the actual ticket price, which still comes in under $25 with tax, also includes the tip. This is a *Best Bargain,* for sure.

The Andy Williams Moon River Theater

Location   2500 W. Highway 76 at Wildwood Drive, across from the Grand Palace

Open   April through mid-December

Type of Show   Musical variety concert

Showtimes   Monday–Saturday, 3 and 7 p.m. (September through December only)

Ticket Prices $34 adult; $17 children ages 2–12

Other Shows on Site   Broadway on Ice

Showtimes   Monday through Saturday, 3 and 7 p.m. (April through August only)

Ticket Prices $34 adults; $17 children ages 2–12

Reservations and Information   (417) 334-4500

Dark   Sundays

Seating Capacity   2,000

Disabled Access   Good

Overall Rating   ★★★

General Description   Andy Williams's Moon River Theater is still coolly elegant, a high-gloss oak and mahogany amphitheater accented with some sophisticated art, Navajo rugs, antique silk Japanese Bridal kimonos, and teal-and-terracotta carpeting. It goes a little more Hollywood outside: A "moon river" pond stocked with carp, Japanese koi, and lily pads winds along the side of the building beneath latex and concrete "cliffs." The gift shop seems more elegantly discreet than most, set off by itself like a boutique; but Williams does some selling of his own, talking up the McGuffey's diner next door (he's the landlord), for example. In September and October, Glen Campbell joins Andy on stage, which ups the ticket price $5.

The seating is one-story but very wide-winging—more than 2,000 seats, in what might almost be considered a half-moon shape—with good visibility except at the extreme left and right. The seats themselves deserve a very high comfort ranking. Wheelchair parking is along the transverse aisle parallel to the stage about halfway back, but the rows behind are canted up; just skip the first row or ask to move to the inner rows across the aisle.

Tips: That central aisle is extremely long, and the staff will carefully light your way with flashlights. So if you don't want everybody staring at you, either make sure to use the restrooms before the show or try to time your escape between numbers. Carpeting supplies good traction inside; sound and lighting are first-rate. Special features include Braille signage, earsets for the hearing impaired. The parking lot slopes down fairly sharply in the rear; it would be a good idea to "cluster" plan the day and try to park either at McGuffey's next door (see restaurant listings) or the Grand Palace or Grand Village shops and walk over at sidewalk level. Or, drop off wheelchair users at the main entrance before parking.

The Show   Andy Williams, Shoji Tabuchi, and Mel Tillis are frequently touted (in co-op advertisements) as "Branson's Big Three," with reference to style as well as reputation. Williams, who was the first major non-country performer to take up permanent residence in Branson, still has a fine voice and an almost unmatched ability to connect with the audience, but seems a little on the defensive about having given up country music for pop. One of his medleys zigzags between Nashville and Hollywood, with dueling sets of backup vocalists, though the pop standards are clearly better suited to his vocal styling. His ten years on television tell in the smooth, but not frenetic, rhythm of the show; and the show begins with a classic TV visual joke involving a Williams look-alike in the spotlight. Williams tosses out a lot of age jokes—he seems to be in a friendly duel of barbs with Pat Boone. He uses a full orchestra, and a good one, and knows how to milk a song. Like Tabuchi's show, this mixes in a bit of everything his audience remembers, from the big band and Broadway to biggest hits. Perhaps the one miscalculation is the gospel medley, with full choir; Williams's silky stylings just don't suit the music. There is little kids' interest here, though older children may find it entertaining. Otherwise, a *Best Bargain.*

Other Show   *Broadway On Ice,* the famous ice-skating touring troup, will be featured at the Moon River Theater for the 2000 season. First-rate performances by well-known Olympians such as Tara Lipinski, Katarina Witt, Ty and Randy, and Scott Hamilton make this show a sure bet.

Part Six

Theme Parks, Museums, and Other Attractions

Remedial Treatment for Show Overload

Aside from the entertainment venues, Branson offers a variety of things to see, do, and, of course, buy. If you consider shopping a form of entertainment, check out the "Shopping" chapter later in this book.

The major choices include theme parks, which combine rides and exhibits with concessions, etc.; sightseeing tours and cruises, which may or may not include meals; museums and novelty exhibits; and a few simple novelties. There are also a couple of attractions, most notably White Water and the $40- million Thunder Road, that are purely recreational and have extremely high kids' and teens' appeal but less to offer older adults and seniors.

The profiles that follow are not all as in-depth as the theater venues (except for the two theme parks), since these are really "alternatives" to the music shows. However, the profiles will provide the facts you need to arrange the best trip for your particular group. We'll compare the cost and likely entertainment value for various age groups, the comfort factor, and the quality of the exhibit or attraction. We'll also supply a few tips and tricks for getting the most out of your choices.

Some of these alternate attractions require a greater investment of time than others; Silver Dollar City, for example, the largest of the two theme parks, can keep a whole family occupied for a couple of days on a leisurely visit. Most folks, however, spend one whole day, in which case the $33 admission is really a bargain. Food and souvenirs, of course, will increase that figure. You may not wish to buy tickets for a concert, or much else, for that matter, on the day you're going to the City. Shepherd of the Hills and White Water, on the other hand, may use up half a day, but you probably will want to plan something else as well. Most of the other attractions you can see in an hour or two.

In addition to the attractions, a variety of tours are available. Some tours purely for sightseeing, such as the Branson Scenic Railway, may be more suitable to adults. Others (such as the *Sammy Lane* Pirate Cruise or Ride the Ducks) combine a little excitement that makes them a better family bet. Several of the cruises include meals, which makes them possible "cramming" candidates as well as a way to relax after walking around. And a few, to be honest, are overhyped and/or overpriced.

The Big Two

SILVER DOLLAR CITY

The biggest and most professionally run of the two parks, and a *Best Bargain* pick as well, is Silver Dollar City, which belongs to the company that owns the White Water park and the *Branson Belle* showboat. About nine miles from Branson proper, it used an old regional attraction, Marvel Cave, as a tourist "hook" and opened in 1960 as a small Ozarks village recreation park with a steam-engine train ride, shops, crafts, and musical performances. It still has much the same look—an 1880s or 90s mountain town, with a little farming, a little mining, a little Wild West saloon hallooing and a lot of music—but it has grown considerably.

The park includes about a dozen rides, nearly 50 shops, a dozen restaurants with a variety of "home-cooked" Southern food (barbecue, miner's stew, red beans and rice, fried chicken, all-you-can-eat buffets, and so forth), plus a diet-busting variety of concessions ranging from fragrant hot-apple fritters to ice cream and strawberries. There are six sit-down entertainment areas, several other less formal stages and walking-around music, as well as a new thousand-seat Opera House with concerts and a 3,000-seat outdoor amphitheater called Echo Hollow, where every night a mixed cast of park performers counts down the *Top 100 Country Songs of All Time* (in about two hours). The Echo Hollow concerts begins 15 or 20 minutes after the park itself closes; the amphitheater is at the outer edge of the park and can be closed off.

Tips: Although the park is actually a large circle, the paths seem to wander all over and back—something like drawing a sunflower's petals. Remember that downhill generally leads further into the City; uphill leads you back toward the entrance. Be sure to get one of the maps with number-coded attractions and landmarks. You can go through the park in any direction, but if you first head left, and then move in a roughly clockwise direction (the entrance is at about 7 o'clock), you'll walk down the steeper grade and back up the gentler slope at the end of the day, when you'll probably be tired. Speaking of which: although the several parking lots are somewhat removed from the park itself, shuttle vehicles operate fairly constantly. You may, however, have to wait a while in line, without shelter. We found the five-minute walk to the entrance preferable.

The "cast" and staff of the park are not only dressed in costume, they "live" their roles as farmers, craftsmen, cooks, showgirls, etc. in the 1890s. The keeper of the hen house, one of the best actors in the park (a former Kansas City executive who discovered he hated retirement), will show kids how to feed animals or gather eggs. Any of the jewelers, paper makers, candlemakers, woodcarvers, etc., will tell you as much or more than you want to know about their business (and where the closest restrooms are, etc.). Kids are allowed to participate in several crafts, including dipping candles, pulling taffy, and making a bowl on the pottery wheel. Interestingly, the park management follows a seniority system in allocating craft booth locations; the more long-standing ones are closer in (and lower on the hill), the junior artisans are up higher and farther away. *Tip:* "Granny's" real lye soap, boiled in a cauldron and sold in bars, is a great antidote for poison ivy and insect bites—which may be a less welcome souvenir of Branson—and very cheap. There are special festivals at the park during the season, including a quilt festival in late summer and a national crafts festival in fall.

A brand new "Liquid Coaster" was opened for the 1999 season. Buzz-saw Falls combines a fun water ride with a thrilling roller coaster experience. Among the other rides are a roller coaster called the Thunderation (major thrill—speeding backwards), Huck Finn's Tree House (similar to the Disney model but pretty nice), a flume ride, and the railroad excursion, which is frequently, one might even (ahem) say regularly, interrupted by six-gun slinging bandits. Several involve splashing water, so don't wear anything that stains. If you are really worried about getting wet, cut head and arm holes in a plastic trash bag and wear it on the water rides like a sack dress.

Silver Dollar City opened the brightly colored "World's Largest Tree House" in 1997. Younger children will get a kick out of the three-story structure which is decked out with swinging bridges, all kinds of gadgets, and a giant geyser. *Tip:* Make sure the kids wear comfortable shoes with good traction. Although the tree house is completely safe, kids may get wet, and they will have more fun if they can run and jump around with ease.

Don't forget old faithful: Marvel Cave, which has 32 miles of explored passages and a huge main room 20 stories high. A cable railway returns visitors to the cave entrance, which is just inside the turnstiles and sometimes gets overlooked by kids straining at the bit.

The ten shows range from rotating outdoor old-timey and folkish performances in the Gazebo to ragtime and Dixieland, hillbilly, Cajun, and the informal can-can show, complete with Irish tenor and barrelhouse pianist, in the (nonalcoholic, of course) Silver Dollar Saloon. The Opera House hosts large production shows. In high season, you may have to stand in line for a scheduled indoor show. However, all musical events, including the two-hour Echo Hollow show, are included in the admission price.

Tip: The Gazebo amphitheater, which is fairly near the front entrance and at the junction of several of the walkways, is a good place to meet back up if the party wants to split up and go to different places. However, really lost or misplaced family members are led by staff to the Train Depot, near the children's ride cluster called Tom Sawyer's Landing.

Special features include an automatic teller machine, mobile TDD machines for the hearing impaired, and in-and-out admission on the same day (if you get your hand stamped at the exit before leaving). Since the parking is free anyway, you may choose to take a break to change clothes, get in a cooling swim, etc. Customer relations here are excellent, and complaints and emergencies well-handled. Pets are allowed on leashes, and water for pets is available at any food site.

Super Saver

As mentioned, there are extended passes for the park. A season pass is $55 for adults and $45 for children (including tax). However, if you aren't sure how much time you want to spend at the park, you can test the waters, so to speak: buy one-day tickets and then "trade up" to a vacation or season pass by turning in your ticket stub (on the day you buy it only) for full credit toward the season-pass price at the Exchange Booth, the General Store, or several other locations. The season pass allows you to bring guests at a discounted price and buy tickets to the Grand Palace or White Water amusement park at a discount as well. There are also combination passes, one day at the City and one day at White Water and other Silver Dollar City–owned attractions which can save you 10–20%.

Operating Hours

Silver Dollar City, on Highway 265 just south of the 76 intersection, is open from mid-April until nearly Christmas, with a short break early in November to decorate for Old Time Country Christmas. General hours of operation: April through October, 9:30 a.m. to 6 p.m., and November through December, 1 to 10 p.m.

One-Day Admission

$33 plus tax adult, $31 ages 55 and up, $23 children ages 4–11, under 4 free. Parking and tax included in ticket price. Call (800) 952-6626 or (417) 338-8210.

SHEPHERD OF THE HILLS

On the site of the family farm that inspired Wright is Shepherd of the Hills Homestead, part recreation, part theme park and part theatrical venue. It has some steep walkways, although everything can be done by tram; in particular, the walk to the amphitheater can be tough even going downhill, so be sure to wear shoes with resistant soles.

There are a small number of artisan and craft shops, plus a couple of restaurants on site. The wagon maker, Earl Maggard, who keeps all the homestead and theater vehicles in operating condition, also hand-crafts two-seater buggies and larger carriages to order for horse-owners. Jeep tours, leaving every 30 minutes and lasting about an hour, go to Old Matt's Cabin, his mill, Little Pete's Cave, and Jennings' Still, and to the amphitheater for some old-timey entertainment. Old Matt's Cabin, built in 1884, has a sweet confusion of artifacts—pump organ, books, lattice-back chairs, and rifles over the fireplace, plus a back porch with a loom and utensils—but is locked up and only opened by the tour guides: no self-service. A pretty little chapel, built in 1901 and moved to Branson a couple of years ago, is under-visited and a nice place to think.

Among kids' attractions are a smallish playground, Clydesdale wagon rides, horseback rides (fairly tame), and a barn full of champion miniature horses and mules (not recommended for petting). Among the boutiques is a "Precious Moments" shop, featuring the spaniel-eyed prepubescent angels of artist Samuel J. Butcher, who has decorated an entire chapel—ceiling to floor—in Carthage, Missouri, about two hours away.

On the knoll where Wright made his campsite, called Inspiration Point, is a 230-foot tower with a panoramic view from two levels, one open-air with coin binoculars and one with glass, directional plaques, and *Shepherd* quotations. It's a good view of the area, but frankly, there isn't all that much to see—woods, hills, and bald knobs. The Bald Knobbers are acknowledged, but described here as a "secret law-and-order group." The scenic views along the Clydesdale route are just as good, and included in the price. During Ozark Mountain Christmas, the tower has a good view of the area lights. At the foot of the tower are an oversized flower-bed clock that chimes, a huge sundial, and statues of the characters from the novel.

The park also holds an 1,500-seat outdoor amphitheater, where a dramatic version of *Shepherd,* complete with live horses, a bonfire, and guns, is performed after dark by a cast of about 90. A full-length (approximately two hours with intermission) production, it reportedly moves some people greatly, but it is produced in an old-fashioned and very melodramatic (read amateurish) manner. It may seem extremely hammy to audiences more used to television and realistic movies than to the old Saturday matinees.

The story, in short, is a morality play: the novel's opening, which is often quoted around town, says, "This, my story, is a very old story . . . the story of a man who took the trail that leads to the lower ground, and of a woman, and how she found her way to the higher sunlit fields." A would-be artist, who has abandoned his pregnant Ozark fiancée, is believed to have died. The fiancée dies in childbirth. The artist's father, a preacher, moves to the Ozarks to find his son but learns the tragic story instead; ashamed, he does not reveal his own identity, but goes into service as Preacher Bob, "the Shepherd of the Hills." As expiation, he helps persuade another young girl, Sammy, not to elope to the city with a swell, but stay with the people—especially the hero, Young Matt—whom she truly loves. Meanwhile, the Bald Knobbers, the local vigilantes and bank robbers who have stolen what was to be the government aid to drought-stricken farmers, decide that Preacher Bob is really a federal agent and try to burn him out. The posse catches up just in time for an elaborate shoot-out. A ghostly figure who has played a role in stopping the Bald Knobbers is revealed, on his deathbed, to be the faithless artist and preacher's son, who had returned for his fiancée but came too late.

Dramatically, this makes for a lot of breast-beating, praying, pulled punches and so on. There is some audience participation—at intermission, patrons are invited to join in the community square dance—and older adults, especially those who loved the book, will like it. The acoustics and sight lines are uniformly good; wheelchair seating is provided and there is a "time-out" room as well. The kids' and young adults' appeal rating may be lower, however. And there is also the problem of the lag time between the homestead's closing and the play's beginning; you'll have to go out and come back. Except for fans of Wright's book, we rank this lowest of the three parks.

During Ozark Mountain Christmas, Santa appears in person and makes for greater family appeal. Shepherd of the Hills also sets up the drive-through *Homestead Trail of Lights* with over 75 areas displaying mechanical elves, Santas, reindeer, and nativity scenes. The trail is impressive due to the sheer number of lights and moving figures and will be especially appealing to kids.

Tip: Signs at the beginning of the trail ask that you use parking headlights only, so keep your eyes on the (dark and narrow) road. We saw a car run off the road and root its right wheels firmly in a ditch while driving the trail.

Special features include tram transportation from the parking lot to the amphitheater (not just for the handicapped). Even though this theater is outdoors, smoking is forbidden.

Operating Hours

Shepherd of the Hills Homestead, on 76 about two miles north of the Shepherd of the Hills Expressway intersection, is open from April through mid-December, daily, 9 a.m. to 5 p.m.

Inspiration Tower is now open year-round (rather than seasonally, as it was in the past), daily from 9 a.m. to 8 p.m.

Shepherd of the Hills is performed late April through mid-August, daily, 8:30 p.m. and September through October, daily, 7:30 p.m.

Admission

Homestead: $13 adults, $7 children ages 4–12, under 4 free; additional tower admission: $5 adults, $2 children ages 4–16, under 4 free.

Theater: $21 adults, $10 children ages 4–12, under 4 free. Package ticket including homestead, tower, and theater: $22 adults, $11 children ages 4–12. Call (417) 334-4191.

Other Attractions

Hollywood Wax Museum

"The eyes have it" at this classic wax museum right on the strip. The wonderful American mish-mash of Hollywood, TV, religion, and politics has an eerie life-like quality thanks to the superior craft of wax artists assembled by the Los Angeles Hollywood Wax facility. Only one figure (look for him—hint: blue tights) fails to reflect a genuine glint in his eye. Making good multi-level use of the cavernous warehouse building decorated on the outside with Mount Rushmore–like mugs of John Wayne, Elvis, Marilyn, and Charlie Chaplin, be sure to look all around as you travel at your own speed through the labyrinth. Roughly plan on 45 minutes. Steps are part of the path, but an elevator is available. Tell them you need it as you enter, or you'll have to backtrack to get help. This attraction has three major advantages: it has appeal for all ages since the figures and dioramas depict everything from popular culture of the 1920s to 1990s; you can use it for an expandable/ contractible "filler" in between shows, meals, etc.; and it is open long hours. Coupons for $1–2 off the admission can easily be found in many brochures. The whole facility is a lot of fun, but the monster children chamber is probably too intense for children under age 8. This descent, which can be circumvented, has an honest supernatural chill to it that can't be explained.

Operating Hours   Hollywood Wax Museum, located at 3030 West Hwy. 76 (near the Osmond Theatre), is open daily from 8 a.m. to midnight, mid-April through mid-December. Closes at 6 p.m. the rest of the year.

Admission $9.95 adults, $6.95 children ages 6–11, free for children ages 5 and under. No reservations needed. For information call (800) 720-4110 or (417) 33-STARS.

Ripley's Believe It or Not! Museum

The most entertaining thing about Ripley's Believe It or Not! Museum is its "architecture," which suggest a plantation home cracked wide open by an earthquake, with gaping holes and shattered plaster. A concrete and metal "fault line" through the lobby floor, an apparently eternal and sourceless column of water, and constant earthquake sound effects complete this tribute to Missouri's frequently unsettled past along the New Madrid fault (a reminder that many other local businesses consider unfortunate at best and at worst, terrible PR).

Most of the exhibits seem pretty tame, however, almost a spoof on the old comic-strip style Ripley's reports. These days, "shrunken heads" and totem poles don't go very far, and no bit of silly excess—not even a glamorous limo with Jacuzzi or that famous "largest ball of twine in the world"—is at all hard to believe. The passage twists and turns to make the exhibits seem more impressive, but succeeds primarily in backing up traffic. It will probably distract kids and maybe teens who don't watch much television; but frankly, we can't recommend it except as a rainy-day fallback.

Operating Hours   Ripley's Believe It or Not! Museum, on 76 a block west of the 165/Gretna Road intersection, is open Monday–Thursday, 9 a.m. to 9 p.m., and Friday and Saturday, 9 a.m. to 10 p.m.

Admission $11.95 adults, $7.45 children ages 4–12. Call (417) 337-5460.

Ralph Foster Museum

The Ralph Foster Museum at College of the Ozarks seems most often to advertise its "celebrity" attraction, namely the jalopy used by the actors in the TV series, *The Beverly Hillbillies,* but it does have quite a bit more to offer—even in auto terms (a 1931 Rolls Royce). Exhibits include a hands-on discovery room and petting zoo for kids; a collection of native American artifacts and stuffed animals (a nine-foot-tall polar bear, which seems like a private competition with the ones at Bass Pro Outdoor World in Springfield); a reconstructed log cabin, barber shop and smithy; some Depression glass, art glass, scrimshaw, and furniture. This emphasis on handcrafts, and the moved and rebuilt 1864 schoolhouse alongside the museum, seem symbolic of the whole campus, because the College of the Ozarks at large is maintained partly by student labor (part of their tuition fee) and souvenir sales of handmade textiles, jellies and baskets as well as meal from the operating grist mill. There is also a 6,000-orchid greenhouse. This is a much better bargain, educationally and financially, than Ripley's.

Operating Hours   The Ralph Foster Museum at College of the Ozarks, on country road V about a mile off Highway 65 across the river from Old Downtown Branson, is open year-round, Monday–Friday, 9 a.m. to 4:30 p.m.

Admission $4.50 adults, $3.50 ages 62 and up, 18 and under free. Call (417) 334-6411.

Boxcar Willie Museum

The Boxcar Willie Museum stands in the parking lot of the Dutton Family Theater (formerly the Boxcar Willie Theatre). A collection of the Branson legend's memorabilia is on display.

Operating Hours   Monday through Saturday, April through December

Admission $3 per person. Call (417) 334-8696.

Stone Hill Winery

Missouri may not be famous as a wine-making state, but Branson's Stone Hill Winery has begun accumulating a lot of awards at wine competitions, and some of the wines are very good. A range of white, red, and sparkling wines, from sweet to fruity to dry, are on sale, and free tours and tastings run continuously. (Kids get grape juice.) The winemaking staff is generally young but very knowledgeable and engaging. Along with the wines, which can either be shipped to your home or carried out, wine paraphernalia and gifts are for sale. Case discounts and follow-up shipping are also available.

Operating Hours   Stone Hill Winery, on 165 two blocks south of the 76 intersection, is open year-round, Monday–Saturday, 8:30 a.m. to 6 p.m., and Sunday, 11 a.m. to 6 p.m. Call (417) 334-1897.

Ozarks Discovery IMAX Theater

This is a six-story-tall movie screen that produces lifelike, sometimes dizzyingly realistic, films ten times the size of the usual image. The 50-minute $3.5 million presentation, "Ozarks: Legacy & Legend," will be a main feature here "for at least ten years," according to an IMAX marketing official. Shot locally and with mostly local talent, the film blends the natural, political, and social history of the area with its folklore and values in a saga of six generations of the McFarlain family from 1824–1950. Suitable for children and adults, the aerial footage of the Ozarks landscape especially is a nice complement to the constructed reality of Branson. As with all IMAX presentations, the best seats are in the center of the house. A demonstration of the superior IMAX technology with 44 speakers, "yadda-yadda-yadda," and hosted by the voice of Jim Stafford enhances the appreciation of the main experience. Other alternating feature films include "Supernova," "The Living Sea," "Everest," "Alaska, Spirit of the Wild," and "Grand Canyon." Holiday features include a version of "The Nutcracker." Call in advance to determine which one accompanies the ongoing "Ozarks" film screened everyday at 9 a.m., 11 a.m., noon, 3 p.m., and 5 p.m. If you save your first ticket stub, its worth a 50% discount for a second show within the same week. Also in the IMAX complex are shops and food.

Operating Hours   IMAX, on Shepherd of the Hills Expressway between the Shoji Tabuchi and *Country Tonite!* theaters, is open year-round.

Admission $8 adults, $7.50 ages 60 and over, $5 children ages 3–12. Shows hourly. Phone (417) 335-4832 for showtimes.

White Water

A swimming and sunning theme park subtitled "Tropical Adventures in Paradise," White Water is a vast wet playground. There are 12 acres of slides, flumes, tunnels, a 200-foot plunge, a rapids ride, a wave pool (called the Surfquake), and for the tamer temperament, a float pool. This is guaranteed to keep kids happy, and on a hot day, their parents as well. It's not cheap, but it can be made more economical by purchasing vacation passes, Silver Dollar City combo tickets, etc.

Operating Hours   White Water, 3305 W. Hwy 76 near Gretna Road, is open late-May through August, daily from 9 a.m. to 8 p.m. Phone (417) 334-7487 or (417) 336-7100.

Admission   Whole day passes are $25 for adults, $19 for children ages 4–12, and $11 for ages 55 and over. Afternoon splash passes, good only after 4 p.m., are less expensive. Season passes are $45 for adults and $35 for children; combination tickets for one day at Silver Dollar City and one day at White Water are $52 for adults and $35 for children ages 4–11, a family best bet.

Waltzing Waters

This attraction is all wet—but not the in way the press release would have you believe. The show combines 40,000 gallons of water, a lot of colored lights, and musically synchronized fountains. It's not fascinating, but it's not expensive either.

Operating Hours   Waltzing Waters, on 76 between Gretna Road and

Shepherd of the Hills Expressway, is open daily March through December, 9 a.m. to 10 p.m.

Admission $6 adults, $3 children under age 12. Phone (417) 334-4144. Frederick Antonio plays two pianos at once in front of the fountains, Tuesday–Sunday at 10 a.m., 1 p.m., and 6 p.m. Admission to Frederick is $12 for adults and $6 for children under age 12.

Cruises, Tours, and Sightseeing

Ride the Ducks

As mentioned in "Getting In, Getting Around," the amphibious tour called "Ride the Ducks" is a good way to get a glimpse of some of the other, meaning non-musical, tourist attractions. The Ducks themselves, chunky vehicles that resemble power boats with decapitated shuttle vans stuck on top, not only tour the military vehicle graveyard, as mentioned, but also chug along to Table Rock Dam and stop off at Shepherd of the Hills trout farm, which may seem like a shortcut into the wilderness but which many sportsmen seem to revere.

Tips: The elevated rear rows, which stick out from behind the canopy, can be attractive to those who like a little sun, especially while the Duck drifts through the water. However, the breeze can be stiff, and when the Duck launches off the banks into Table Rock Lake, there is usually at least some splashing. The captain will invite anyone who wants to, generally the children but occasionally an adult, to steer the ship while it's in the lake. The tour lasts about 70 minutes.

At the beginning of the tour, the entire bus will be photographed by an assistant; although the captain jokes that the pictures are meant to tell him later if anyone's fallen off, you will actually be invited to buy the photo as a souvenir. Admittedly, it's a better photo set-up than some of those that ambush you at the theaters, and it produces an oversized print in which you may well be recognizable, but it still costs $5 if you want a copy. *Tip:* Ride the Ducks has probably the greatest number of show and attraction discount coupons in Branson, so keep your eyes open.

Hours and Admission Ride the Ducks, 2320 W. Highway 76 east of the Grand Palace, is open daily, mid-March through mid-December, 8 a.m. to 5 p.m. Adult passage $13.44, children $6.70. Phone (417) 334-3825.

Branson Scenic Railway

The rail ride is an excursion more than a tour, a 40-mile round trip aboard a trio of beautifully restored old observation cars with vista-view domes and one club car. It travels across a mile-long, 600-foot-high wooden trestle and along the hillsides to Harrison and back. *Tip:* There is no turn-around—the train "reverses" all the way back to Branson—so the thing to do is get into the rear of the last car, which has a curved window bay, and wait for the ride back to see everything. All cars are non-smoking.

Hours and Admission   The Branson Scenic Railway departs from the Main Street depot in Old Downtown Branson near the waterfront, mid-March through mid-December at 9 and 11:30 a.m. and 2 p.m. June through early August and October there is also a 5 p.m. departure. Saturday night dinner rides are also available. Adult passage $21, children ages 3–12 $10. Saturday dinner rides are $46.71. Call (417) 334-6110 or (800) 2-TRAIN-2.

Tablerock Helicopters

For those who prefer the aerial view to the rail view, Tablerock Helicopter tours take off from the helipad at 3309 Highway 76 near Gretna Road and swing over the Strip down to Table Rock Lake and Dam, Shepherd of the Hills Trout Hatchery, Indian Point, and Eureka Springs. Passage $17.95 and up, lap children free. Phone (417) 334-6102 or Web site www.table-rockhelecopters.com.

Sammy Lane Pirate Cruise

This is one of the state's oldest continuous attractions, going back to 1913. The "Sammy Lane" memorialized is actually a she, the young heroine of *Shepherd of the Hills.* The cruise is 70 minutes long and includes not only a narrated history of the White River but a stop at the old Boston Ride gold mine and an attempted "hijacking" by an eye-patched pirate "sailing" a dragon-headed ship with cannon. Kids' appeal is high, especially as children are invited both to steer the boat and defeat the pirate.

Hours and Admission   The *Sammy Lane* Pirate Cruise, which leaves from Downtown Branson at the foot of Main Street, operates from late April through mid-October. Several departures a day; call for schedules. Admission: $10.95 adults, $7 children ages 3–12, under age 3 free. Call (417) 334-3015 or Web site www.bransoncruises.com.

Lake Queen Pirate Cruise

Sister ship to the *Sammy Lane,* the *Lake Queen* is a handsome old paddle-wheeler offering buffet breakfast (9:30 a.m.) and dinner (5 p.m.) cruises, with live entertainment, as well as four sightseeing tours in the afternoon.

Adult fares range from $12 to $22, children $13. The *Lake Queen* sails from April through mid-December. Call (417) 334-3015.

Polynesian Princess

This float trip cruises Table Rock Lake, with a 90-minute 10 a.m. sightseeing tour ($12) and 5 and 8 p.m. dinner cruises with "Polynesian" entertainment ($27). It sails from Gage's Long Creek marina off US 65.

Part Seven

Restaurants and Dining

Branson Dining:
À la Carte vs. All You Can Eat

Although most guidebooks in the *Unofficial Guide* series have extensive reviews of restaurants and nightclubs, we felt that dining out was less a part of the vacation experience in Branson than elsewhere. First of all, the majority of restaurants are either buffet or chain operations catering to family groups and tours. Second, as we mentioned in the introduction, Branson does not yet have much of a late-night scene—although, as some far-sighted theater owners have begun to realize, it will be important over the next several years for the town to develop more attractions for young singles.

In this chapter we describe a sampler of restaurants, ranging from the nicest (Devil's Pool at Big Cedar Lodge) to the homiest (Branson Cafe), a few theater tie-ins (Mickey Gilley's Cafe and Pie-Annie's at Jim Stafford's), some good buffet possibilities (Welk's Stage Door Canteen), suprisingly good sushi (Shogun), and a couple of local favorites.

There are a few general things to know. First, the longtime Kansas City–Ozarks connection means that there is a lot of meat, and it's almost uniformly high-quality. If you like prime rib, Branson is a good place to be. (On the other hand, the word "barbecue" in Branson just means ribs, not pulled meat; and usually pork ribs only.) A lot more seafood is being flown in, iced but not frozen, so broiled and grilled seafood dishes are more dependable than they used to be. Finally, although there is a lot of Tex-Mex cooking in town, including tortilla chips and salsa dip in the bars, hot spices have not made much of a dent in Branson palates yet. If you like your chilies strong, ask for the pepper sauce.

All of the restaurants profiled below are wheelchair-accessible; all except the Branson Cafe have nonsmoking sections.

Again, if you are used to the prices at most vacation destinations, you may be surprised here. Note that in our restaurant profiles, "inexpensive" means that entrees are generally under $10, "moderate" means entrees are between $10 and $15 and "expensive" means entrees are generally $15 or over. The "overall rating" evaluates the restaurant's ambitions as well as its execution—that is, something like the Branson Cafe, which doesn't pretend to be anything other than what it is, gets a "very good" rating, even though it's not fancy food. Devil's Pool gets a "very good" rating, too, but the food there is more elaborate and more expensive—it has to be worth it. Some places are only "fair" either because they charge too much for what they provide or just because the food is only . . . fair.

BUFFET FARE PLAY

While it is true that buffets are "all you can eat," it is rather inconsiderate to try to prove how much that is all at once. If you overload your plate, rather than planning to come back for a second helping, chances are somebody in line will miss out on that dish before it can be replaced. Also, don't lean in under the sneeze guard to examine something or try to reach a dish on the other side of the counter; the glass is there not only to keep food warm, but to keep it reasonably hygienic.

If you aren't sure exactly what you want, you might stand a little away and look the table over before getting in line; that way you won't hold other people up. And in Branson particularly, keeping the line moving is important, since people are almost always on their way to a scheduled performance—often in tour group numbers. (This suggests you should avoid buffets from, say, 11:30 to 1 at lunch and 5:30 to 7 at night.)

There are usually separate piles of plates at each buffet table (salad, fruit, dessert, etc.). Once a plate is dirty, it's more polite to leave it on your table and pick up a clean one for your next course. Finally, even though you are serving yourself, you are almost certainly being served your beverage by a waiter or waitress; don't forget to leave a tip.

Branson Cafe

Cuisine   Home-style cooking
Cost   Inexpensive
Overall Rating   Very good
Address   120 West Main Street
Telephone   (417) 334-3021
Atmosphere   Family-style

Dress   Informal

Open   Monday–Saturday, 5:30 a.m.–8 p.m.

The Branson Cafe is one of those down-home kitchens every town used to have a lot of, and now usually has just one hidden away that only the real regulars know about. The Branson Cafe is the town regulars' hangout—it still has a table for the morning gossip circle and a shelf of their mugs—but it handles tourist traffic with aplomb and unruffled country humor.

The best thumbnail proof of this kitchen's authenticity are the biscuits (no trace of powder), the jams, and the desserts (as many as three cobblers, five pies, and a shortcake in a single day, and each pie with a meringue as high as Lyle Lovett's hair). Coffee is 65 cents with infinite refills, and it's good coffee. There is a fair amount of smoking going on, which may surprise you after the smoke-free theaters over on the strip. The food here is pretty good: nobody's ever disputed the signs that read, "If the Colonel had our [fried chicken] recipe, he'd be a general now!"

B. T. Bones

Cuisine   Steak and barbecue

Cost   Moderate to expensive

Overall Rating   Good

Address   Shepherd of the Hills Expressway at Gretna Road

Telephone   (417) 335-2002

Atmosphere   Singles bar

Dress   Casual to slightly dressy

Open   Monday–Saturday, 11 a.m.–1 a.m.; Sunday, 11 a.m.–midnight

This is one of the few nightspots with live music—usually pretty good local country and C&W talent—and dancing. It also has pretty good food, and with more options than there may seem to be at first. The decor is very ranchero, and the prime rib and fajitas are the house favorites (the kitchen's special gimmick is lemon pepper on the beef); but there is a lot of grilled fish and seafood, including shrimp, trout, catfish, mahi-mahi, and salmon, along with some quail and chicken. The bar is raised slightly (for prime viewing of the dance floor, presumably) and stocked with those elbow-high tables. The bar menu has the typical finger food, such as nachos and "Texas bullets," their name for stuffed and fried jalapeños. Bones is particularly popular with younger singles, and since it stays open late, it also gets a fair number of the locals who work elsewhere. The outdoor waiting area, or "corral," is nice in the evenings.

Buckingham's Restaurant and Oasis

Cuisine   Modern continental

Cost   Expensive

Overall Rating   Fair to good

Address   Palace Inn, Highway 76; next to the Grand Village

Telephone   (417) 337-7777

Atmosphere   Retro-safari club

Dress   Business, nice casual

Open   Monday–Saturday, 5–9 p.m.; lounge opens at 1 p.m.; closed, Sunday.

Buckingham's looks like a Hollywood decorator's memory of a glam-era living room: animal skin prints and carved wooden totems and date palms. The menu is rather strenuously clever, and not always well considered. One of the house specials is a lobster stuffed with jalapeños, wrapped in bacon, broiled and then "finished" with a coffee barbecue sauce, by which time any lobster flavor is finished for sure. In general, the simpler the matchups the better: stick to the venison medallions, the mesquite-smoked duck, the grilled tuna, or the smoked pork tenderloin. Prime rib here is good, and offered in three sizes. Several of the appetizers, incidentally, might serve as light fare: for example grilled "tai," presumably meaning "Thai" shrimp, pan-seared quail with Grand Marnier, and the smoked trout.

Salads are heavily dressed, and the desserts are extremely rich. There is a tendency to flambé a lot of things, from steak Diane to "bananas fosters" (sic) to coffee. Don't use too much hairspray.

Buckingham's has only recently begun to have a critical audience, and things are likely to improve. Incidentally, although the restaurant closes at 9, the small but pretty lounge stays open until 11, and the wine list is quite good.

Cakes 'n' Cream Dessert Parlor

Cuisine   Pizza, hot dogs, and diner desserts

Cost   Inexpensive

Overall Rating   Very good

Address   2805 W. Hwy. 76, next to Baldknobbers Jamboree

Telephone   (417) 334-4929

Atmosphere   50s ice cream parlor

Dress   Casual

Open   Daily, 10 a.m. to midnight (March through December)

Two (berry-stained) thumbs up for the fact that this little diner exists. Most restaurants in Branson are already shuttered by the time you make it out of the parking lot of that last show of the day. The only alternatives seem to be pre-fab, straight-from-the-freezer-to-the-griddle Denny's-type places.

If you're looking for a fresh, homemade, midnight snack, we recommend Cakes 'n' Cream. They can satisfy your craving for a savory slice of warm, completely homemade, hand-tossed pizza ($3.25 per large slice) or go for broke with a warm bowl of blackberry cobbler (made fresh daily) complete with a scoop of vanilla bean ice cream ($3) and a hot cup of fresh decaf (80 cents). 11:15 at night just doesn't taste this good anywhere else in town. They also offer malts, shakes, banana splits, and hot dogs, to name just a few other temptations.

This is not a place for hours of thoughtful lingering, however. The retro décor is cozy and welcoming, but the line snaking out the door and around the building may make you feel a little guilty for taking up valuable seating once you're finished. But the service is speedy and friendly, much more so than the aforementioned Denny's.

Devil's Pool

Cuisine   Modern regional American

Cost   Expensive

Overall Rating   Very good

Address   Big Cedar Lodge Resort (off 265)

Telephone   (417) 335-5141

Atmosphere   Lavish country lodge

Dress   Informal to dressy

Open   Restaurant open daily, 7 a.m.–2 p.m. and 5–9:30 p.m. Buzzard Bar open daily, 11 a.m.–11 p.m.

This is easily the best restaurant in the area (the whole resort complex, in fact, is the nicest in the entire region). The scenery is spectacular—you should walk the bridge over Devil's Pool from the parking lot—and the lodge itself impeccably designed, with no-two-alike wrought iron animals on the veranda fence, American Arts & Crafts movement details, plank floors and stonework. Although it has been vastly expanded from its 1920 beginnings (which were pretty extravagant even then, since it was the summer home of a pair of railway and manufacturing millionaires), the additions are equally impressive. The main room has a bar at one end and a huge fireplace at the other, with a spectacular view out the long side.

The food would easily hold its own in a big city, where the prices would be considered extremely moderate; they're scarcely over the "expensive" line even here. The menu includes smoked trout and wall-eyed pike presented together, marinated quail, grilled lamb, medallions of venison, and seared scallops with pasta. The few more traditional dishes, such as stuffed pork chops and turkey and even meatloaf, are taken just as seriously. The restaurant also has good homemade bread and extremely good service.

Note: Reservations are accepted for dinner only, and during high season we strongly recommend them.

Downstairs is a less formal lounge called the Buzzard Bar, with another fireplace, a collection of stuffed wild animals, lighter fare, and live music on weekends. It has a veranda that overlooks the swimming pool and the riverfront villas.

Dimitri's Casual Gourmet Dining

Cuisine   Greek and continental

Cost   Expensive

Overall Rating   Good

Address   500 East Main Street (on the waterfront)

Telephone   (417) 334-0888

Atmosphere   White linen and fairly elegant

Dress   Dressy, informal

Open   Daily, 5–10 p.m.

This is a pretty place—a floating restaurant, in fact, with a walkway around three sides and a nice view of the water, and a rather theatrical Grecian formula foyer. (Not that theatrical is inappropriate in this town.) Some of the food is quite good, particularly the charcoal broiled octopus, the seafood fettuccini, the lamb chops (a little too charred, perhaps), and the kebabs. The spaghetti Dimitri-style, with olive oil, feta, and Middle Eastern spices, is a nice change. The fried dishes are fairly dependable, including the veal and catfish; the abalone is often chewy. Like Buckingham's, Dimitri's has an old-fashioned flair for flambé desserts.

There are some disturbing bits of either carelessness or sharp business practices here that should be pointed out: a more expensive wine brought for the one ordered without the price difference being explained, and a minimum of $10 a person in the dining room. Considering that the prices are as high and sometimes higher than those at the Devil's Pool—steak Diane for two is $60—the charges should be straightforward. Also, a 15 percent gratuity is added into the bill, which is common elsewhere, but unusual in Branson, so remember. Service is good, but a little condescending—something that also may have been fashionable 20 years ago, but no longer; and in this town, it really sticks out.

Gilley's Texas Cafe

Cuisine   Tex-Mex

Cost   Moderate

Overall Rating   Good

Address   Highway 76, next to the Mickey Gilley Theater

Telephone   (417) 335-2755

Atmosphere   Family-style, singles bar

Dress   Casual

Open   Daily, 11 a.m.–midnight

This is an easy-going and fairly predictable menu, but the portions are extremely generous—a combo plate of baked beans and potato salad with barbecued ribs and some hot chilies at $11.95 is enough for two. The green chili burrito would stuff Godzilla, though he might want some extra hot sauce. The regular salsas are middlingly spicy only, but if you ask, the staff can give you some Gilley custom pepper sauces that are much more interesting. Their tortilla chips are pretty good, too. This is one of the few places that offer rib eyes, sirloins, and New York strip steaks rather than the often over-marbled and over-blackened prime rib; the steaks, incidentally, are mesquite-flavored.

Gilley's gets a lot of tour bus business—not surprisingly, since the cafe faces Moe Bandy and Jim Stafford and is only a parking lane away from The Celebrity and Gilley's—and early evening is a good time to head for the bar instead of the dining room. (The bar staff here is extremely good.) The bar is very pretty, too, with Southwest-style art tiles and bright pastels.

There are a few kid's plates. Possibly because of the tour-group rush, 15 percent is automatically added to bills for parties of eight or more.

Landry's Seafood House

Cuisine   Seafood, steaks, fowl

Cost   Moderate

Overall Rating   Good

Address   2900 West Hwy. 76

Telephone   (417) 339-1010

Atmosphere   Casual elegance

Dress   Casual to dressy

Open   Sunday–Thursday, 11 a.m.–10 p.m.; Friday and Saturday,
11 a.m.–11 p.m.; call for times in January and February.

The chain that began in 1949 in Texas has its Branson franchise perched on the strip with a handsome vista that falls away as you look out the back glass wall. The wine list gives a good idea of the spread of the menu offerings and prices: a glass of Gallo goes for $3.75 and a bottle of Moet "White Star" can be yours for $53.95. Appetizers start at $3.99; a half-dozen Blue Point oysters from the cold waters of New England will set you back $6.99. The most expensive item on the menu is the $17.99 seafood platter. The seafood is the feature, of course, and you can get it fried, broiled, or grilled. The gumbo made with a dark brown roux truly is spicy and extremely delicious. A full bar and a very handsome dessert tray (Bananas Foster at $5.99 is the signature effort) rounds out the completely civilized dining experience.

Lone Star Steakhouse

Cuisine   Steak and barbecue

Cost   Moderate

Overall Rating   Good

Address   201 Wildwood Drive at Green Mountain

Telephone   (417) 336-5030

Atmosphere   Country and Western saloon

Dress   Casual, cowboy

Open   Sunday–Thursday, 11 a.m.–10 p.m.; Friday and Saturday,
11 a.m.–11 p.m.

This is a chain operation, but a cheery one, with peanut shells on the floor, bullhorns on the wall, neon beef signs, and surprisingly good beef—many locals consider this the best steakhouse in town. It's among the most entertaining, in any case: every 20 minutes or so, the waiters and waitresses jump into the aisles (and occasionally onto tables and bar) and do a line dance to *Boot-Scootin' Boogie* or the like. The menu is "real men's meat"—T-bones, sirloins, Delmonico's, filet, all available with a bourbon mesquite sauce—as well as shrimp, chicken, and ribs. Very cheery staff all round, and pretty fast service.

McGuffey's Eclectic Eatery

Cuisine   California eclectic

Cost   Moderate

Overall Rating   Fair to good

Address   Highway 76, between Andy Williams' Moon River Theater and the Grand Palace

Telephone   (417) 336-3600

Atmosphere   Schoolhouse as saloon

Dress   Casual

Open   Monday–Saturday, 11 a.m.–midnight; Sunday, 11 a.m.–11 p.m.

This is the flagship of a local chain of restaurants that use the old *McGuffy's Reader* as a theme and a menu almost as one-size-fits-all as the old one-room schoolhouse it puns on. There are some stir-fries and pasta dishes that suggest the TGI Friday's menu, some blackened fish, and a bit of homestyle dining. In the main, the menu builds expectations beyond the kitchen's ability to deliver. Stick to simple dishes here and avoid the steaks. The early-evening crowd is older, but the bar does a fairly brisk business after curtain time.

There are other McGuffey's: a similar one, but with a constant bar business, on Highway 248 a little east of Shepherd of the Hills Expressway; and a concept diner on Shepherd of the Hills just past the Shenandoah South theater.

Mesquite Charlie's Steaks

Cuisine   Steaks, prime rib

Cost   Moderate

Overall Rating   Fair

Address   2849 Gretna Rd.

Telephone   (417) 334-0498

Atmosphere   Casual, cowboy

Dress   Casual

Open   Sunday–Thursday, 11 a.m.–10 p.m.; Friday and Saturday, 11 a.m.–11 p.m.

"Missouri's largest restaurant" is situated on a high hill set back from its Gretna Road entrance. The structure is so big that you think it must share another operation with the restaurant, but it doesn't. Catering to tour buses more than to individuals, small parties can get lost in the shuffle and the din. A public address system in the foyer constantly calls for the next mass seating to occur. The meals are of passable quality, but the dining atmosphere lacks real ambiance. Even though there is table service, the scale of the rooms suggest a school cafeteria with the attendant hustle and bustle. The kitchen grill is visible from some seats, (considered an "upscale" advance for Branson), but the young men on the line wear a variety of T-shirts and base-ball caps with ponytails sticking through rather than the traditional chef's uniform and hats that such visibility calls for. Cocktails are available. Menu prices run into the mid-teens for steak or prime rib.

Outback Steak & Oyster Bar

Cuisine   Steak and seafood

Cost   Moderate

Overall Rating   Good

Address   1910 Highway 76, near Fall Creek Road

Telephone   (417) 334-6306

Atmosphere   Camping lodge

Dress   Informal

Open   Sunday–Thursday, 11 a.m.–11 p.m.; Friday and
   Saturday, 11 a.m.–midnight

This is one of the oddest, though most successful, complexes in town: it combines this upscale Aussie-motif steakhouse with a very nice clothing store (natural fibers, handmade paper manuscript books, etc.) and a bungee jump. In other words, you can buy new clothes, eat a big dinner—and then jump and throw up all over your outfit.

Whatever the rationale, this is a hearty place, with a nice separate bar and fireplace at one end and an outdoor deck overlooking a pond at the other. Meat is the big draw, and it's laid right out in front, in butcher-style deli cases just inside the front door. (Actually, in warm weather, one worries about that a little.)

It's not all beef, however: some of it is alligator. The "Melbourne Grill" combines emu, lamb, and venison. There are lamb chops and shish kebab, cold-water lobster tails (broiled or smoked), pork chops and grilled fish and shrimp as well as fried oysters in a variety of Rockefeller-type styles. The food is pretty good, but the staff's knowledge is a little limited. You can get beer in a bucket and bread in a miner's pan.

There is a fair amount of late-night business, and a younger clientele than you might expect. This Outback is not connected to the national Outback chain, incidentally, but the concept is similar.

The Pasta Grill

Cuisine   Italian

Cost   Moderate

Overall Rating   Very good

Address   2690 Green Mountain Rd.

Telephone   (417) 337-9882

Atmosphere   Casual, comfortable, and comforting

Dress   Casual

Open   Daily, 11 a.m.–11 p.m.; limited days and hours in January and February.

For travelers who are overcome with the mystery that is Branson, the Pasta Grill provides a familiar touchstone dining experience. The scale of 220-seat eatery decorated with terra-cotta covered walls and a suspended faux grape arbor combine to create an organic looseness and sophistication that is reminiscent of restaurants in larger cities. The Italian menu is a welcome change from the heavy, straightforward "meat vibe" of most places. Lunch specials range from $5.99 for spaghetti Bolognese to $7.99 for linguini with clam sauce and are accompanied by soup or house salad. Dinners add a choice of potatoes or broccoli and range from $11.25 for salsiccia Parmigiano (charcoal broiled Italian sausage baked with tomato sauce, spices, and cheese) to $15.99 for Bistecca Mudiga (lightly breaded and charcoal grilled beef tenderloin in white wine with chopped prosciutto, mushrooms, and cheese). If you are a pasta fan, we must recommend the spiedini ala pollo (marinated, skewered chicken strips, grilled and served on a bed of penne pasta with a spicy sundried tomato sauce) for $10.25. Seating before shows can take 30–40 minutes, so plan ahead. An option is to eat at the bar that is pleasantly not segregated from the main dining room. Excellent martinis can be had. The exceptionally plush bar stools do not have backs, but sitting on them might get you to your show on time. Carry-out is available, as is a full menu until closing, so you can get a fine meal after the show—a rare event, and another reason why the Pasta Grill is a real fine standout in Branson.

Pie-Annie's

Cuisine   Sandwiches and sweets

Cost   Inexpensive

Overall Rating   Good

Address   3440 W. Hwy. 76, upstairs at the Jim Stafford Theater

Telephone   (417) 335-8080

Atmosphere   Soda shop

Dress   Casual

Open   Daily, 11 a.m.–11 p.m.

Pie-Annie's, named for Jim Stafford's wife, Anne, is a great place to pick up a bite to eat before or after the show. The old-fashioned soda shop atmosphere comes from the hand-painted murals and carefully selected antiques chosen by Jim and Anne themselves. Pie-Annie's features lunches, light dinners, and specialty desserts. Both small and large groups can be accommodated. Menu items include various sandwiches, pies, cakes, cobblers, sundaes, and flavored coffees and teas. An added bonus that makes dining here so appealing is that Jim Stafford heads upstairs to Pie-Annie's after every show to sign autographs and do some guitar-picking that can't be fit into his regular show. Other performers from different venues often join Jim to have a little jam session (no pun intended). For more information about the restaurant, check out Jim's website at www.jimstafford.com.

Pzazz

Cuisine   Traditional American

Cost   Inexpensive

Overall Rating   Good

Address   Highway 165, just inside the Pointe Royale gate

Telephone   (417) 335-2798

Atmosphere   Sports bar and grill

Dress   Casual

Open   Daily, 11 a.m.–midnight

Pzazz is notable for two reasons: one, it's about the only place in the Branson area that shows national sports events on a giant-screen television; and two, it's owned by onetime pitching great Jack Hamilton, who pitched a no-hitter in his rookie year as a Phillie (and hit a grand slam, against the Cards). Hamilton himself is usually playing cards in the cocktail lounge in the back (a bar that looks exactly like every other angler's marina bar, somehow); if you want an autograph, ask politely and he'll oblige.

The tables in the restaurant itself are covered with laminated baseball and sports cards; a half-dozen of Hamilton's old uniforms hang on the walls. The food is simple—sandwiches, pizza, burgers, spaghetti and meatballs—but pretty hearty. The breast of turkey sandwich was carved off an actual roasted breast; the Super Bowl pizza has sirloin tips on it. Alcohol is not advertised on the menu, but it's available.

Shogun

Cuisine   Japanese steakhouse and sushi bar

Cost   Moderate to expensive

Overall Rating   Very good

Address   1962 Hwy. 165, just north of the Welk Resort

Telephone   (417) 336-2244

Atmosphere   Traditional rustic Japanese

Dress   Casual

Open   Daily, hours vary by season

In the style of traditional Japanese steakhouses, Shogun has the typical U-shaped, family-style Hibachi tables that seat up to 16 people, where your food is cooked before your eyes by a chef who adroitly flips shrimp tails into the crown of his paper hat. There are six such tables, which will accommodate many families, but only a few tour busses. Therefore, we highly recommend making reservations if you'd like to share one of these tables without a wait. You'll also find several normal-sized, private tables scattered about, where you order off the menu and are served your food by a waiter. You may still order anything on the menu, even if you are sitting at the private tables, but you will not be treated to the chef's show. There are a good number of seats available at the sushi bar as well.

The sushi here is some of the finest that members of our away team have ever eaten (and that's *a lot* of sushi). Presentation is beautiful and the fish is incredibly fresh. If you've never tried sushi, this would be a great place to sample your first roll. The servers can help you choose a piece that won't be too intimidating. Prices for sushi are from $3.25 for a two piece Nigiri to $12.95 for an eight piece Rainbow roll. The Rainbow roll would be our nomination for those of you delving into sushi for the first time. Hibachi table dinners range from $11 for the assorted vegetables to $19 for the Filet Mignon. Lunch combination plates are quite a deal at $7 to $11, and include salad, fried rice, and Japanese noodles. Miso soup fans, be sure to try a bowl here—delectable!

Stage Door Canteen

Cuisine   Traditional buffet

Cost   Moderate

Overall Rating   Good

Address   Route 165, in the Lawrence Welk Champagne Theatre

Telephone   (417) 337-7469

Atmosphere   Wartime canteen

Dress   Casual or informal

Open   Daily, 8:30 a.m.–8 p.m.

This popular tour-group spot has a lavish all-you-can-eat buffet, with two massive steam tables. The lunch buffet offers typical soup, sandwich, and salad fare, with some hot vegetables and a meat choice. The dinner buffet-serves up good quality entrees, including carved meat, poultry, pork, and fish. The salad section is extensive, and there is a wide array of vegetables, potatoes prepared every which way, and rice casseroles. Dessert covers traditional buffet favorites, with the strawberry shortcake and chocolate mousse getting the most attention.

Probably the best thing about the Stage Door Canteen is that it will suit everyone in your group: Dieters, meat-and-threes, vegetarians (though vegans won't find overmuch anywhere in Branson), even Uncle Albert, who won't eat food that's been rolled up in a tortilla, shell, or otherwise "all muddled-up together."

As mentioned in the "Entertainment" chapter, this is the site of one of the best breakfast shows in town, the Lennon Brothers; the combination is a "very good" bargain. There is also dancing and live music here most evenings.

Starlite Diner

Cuisine   Malts, burgers, and chili cheese fries

Cost   Inexpensive

Overall Rating   Good

Address   3115 W. Hwy. 76, inside the Starlite Theatre

Telephone   (417) 337-9333

Atmosphere   50s retro diner

Dress   Casual

Open   Daily, 11 a.m.–9 p.m.

The Starlight Diner may arguably have the best milkshakes in all of Branson. Thick, creamy, eat with a spoon while your legs dangle off the edge of the dock over summer vacation kind of good. No matter how obscure your favorite childhood flavor was, they can likely re-create it. Milkshakes aren't the only decadant treats at Starlite. Sandwiches, soups, and sides come out of the kitchen looking like they did back in the 50s—big, juicy, two-hand, burgers with all the trimmings, bowls of chili large enough to share, and massive sides of beer-battered onion rings that are a meal in themselves.

Though handily tucked into the Starlite Theatre, the Starlight Diner could stand alone on the quality of its tasty food. We recommend you stop in for lunch even if you don't have plans to see a show here. *Tip:* Try the Butterscotch malt. If we could have finished more than the two we ordered, we would gladly be drinking them still.

Uptown Cafe

Cuisine   Traditional American

Cost   Inexpensive

Overall Rating   Good

Address   Highway 165, just south of 76

Telephone   (417) 336-3535

Atmosphere   Deco diner

Dress   Casual

Open   Daily, 7:30 a.m.–midnight

This is undoubtedly one of the most attractive decors in town, blond wood, art Deco chrome touches and sconces, and blue tiles on the soda fountain (which encircles the kitchen, nicely echoing the half-moon exterior). The kitchen does diner food extremely well: fine sandwiches, burgers, meats-and-three, and real soda fountain creations. Diners are a fairly common gimmick in Branson, but this is probably the best. And its iced tea is a blue-ribbon winner—totally restorative on the hottest of days. The staff couldn't be more helpful, either.

Part Eight

Shopping

Souvenirs, Crafts, and Memorabilia

If it's only souvenirs you're looking for, you may confidently skip this section. Every music theater you enter will have plenty of celebrity memorabilia—in fact, you'll be hard pressed to escape without some. Most of the spaces between theaters along the 76 Strip are filled in with mini-clusters of shops. The amusement parks, particularly Silver Dollar City, have scores of craftsmen working on site, and the atmosphere, natural beauty, and variety of crafts at the park make it one of the most enjoyable shopping experiences in Branson. And although Wal-Mart stores are not generally considered tourist attractions, the one in Branson is, because, as the locals say, "it's where the stars shop."

Nevertheless, if you're interested in a little concentrated browsing, here are the major spots. Virtually all are within sight of Highway 76; most of the shopping district of the old town is, too (Highway 76 becomes Main Street a few blocks from the river). There is street parking (diagonal) pretty much all around, and some of the shuttle buses run to Old Downtown as well.

OLD DOWNTOWN BRANSON

There is not a great deal of 19th-century Branson visible, because two great fires in 1912 and 1913 destroyed most of the buildings. The oldest commercial building left is the Branson Hotel on Main Street, one of the earliest tourist accommodations—Harold Bell Wright slept here, of course—and now an attractive bed and breakfast. However, Main Street is a rather pleasant version of early 20th-century small-town brick architecture, including a few old warehouses that have been turned into flea markets and antique malls. There are frequently street fairs and festivals downtown as well.

Downtown is bordered on three sides by a loop of Lake Taneycomo, and the railroad tracks follow much the same curve about two blocks from the waterfront. Branson's Main Street, which is 76 extended, is the primary shopping area; the cross street, about two blocks west of the railroad tracks, is Commercial. (Commercial is one block off Business 65 at Main, then the routes merge.) There is a visitor's information center and one-stop ticket retailer at the corner of Commercial and Main.

Most of the stores are within a small area between the tracks and Business 65; the docks for the cruise lines, the public fishing dock, and the city park are within an easy stroll on either side of where Main Street dead-ends at the water. **The Branson Cafe** at 120 West Main is a landmark (see "Restaurants and Dining").

Among the most popular tourist attractions is **Dick's Oldtime 5 & 10** at 103 West Main, which carries all the traditional dimestore merchandise —embroidery thread, cotton socks and underwear, wrapping paper, magnets, greeting cards, dried flowers, thumbtacks, makeup, candy, and garden tools—and while they may cost more than a dime, it's not a whole lot more. (There is a bakery a few doors up from Dick's that makes not only walnut and pecan sticky buns but cashew buns as well.) The **Branson Mercantile & Co.** on Commercial Street specializes in *Hee-Haw* overalls and jeans in general.

Several antique arcades/flea markets have taken over old buildings along Main Street closer to the railroad tracks. Not surprising, considering the Kewpie connection, there are several shops catering to doll collectors, including **ABC Dolls & Collectibles** at 1149 W. Highway 76. For more information, call the Downtown Branson Business Association at (417) 334-1548.

Incidentally, there is one historical landmark worth looking for: The WPA-era public restrooms, very plain but still serviceable, behind the Burlington shoe outlet at the corner of Commercial and Pacific (the street one block south of Main).

OUTLETS, MALLS, ETC.

The **Grand Village** is an upscale "concept" shopping complex that looks a little like a cross between a Currier & Ives engraving and an Old World movie set, with lots of false balconies and turrets and steeples and prettily landscaped walkways. There are about two dozen shops and a handful of places to eat, including the **Hard Luck Diner,** a 50s-style hamburger and soda shop with singing servers (and cute names like "Achy Breaky Brats"); and the **Village Pantry,** a bakery and California-style sandwich spot. There is a fair amount of nostalgia represented, including a Coca-Cola store, a vintage radio and movies memorabilia collection called "Remember When . . .," the soda counter–style diner, a sports memorabilia shop, and a teddy-bear collection. However, there are also haute Southwestern, sportswear, pet couture, jewelry, and eco-chic boutiques, too. Most merchandise is in the under-$100 range, but there are a few very expensive pieces of art and vintage collectibles.

The Grand Village is logistically important, too, because it's just to the west of the Grand Palace, and has a fair amount of level parking. It's a useful cluster spot for the Andy Williams, Baldknobbers, and Bobby Vinton theaters as well as the Grand Palace. The Grand Village, on 76 at Thousands Hills Road, is open year-round; call (417) 336-7280.

The **Factory Merchants Mall** has more than 90 outlets for such name brands as Corning, Izod, L'Eggs/Hanes, Geoffrey Beene, OshKosh B'Gosh, American Tourister, Bass, Guess, Evan Picone, etc.; there are entrances on Highway 76 (look for the red roofs) and (to the lower level) on Gretna Road. Stores are open year-round, with curtailed hours in January and February; call (417) 335-6686. **Factory Shoppes at Branson Meadows** features apparel, footwear, jewelry, cosmetics, home accessories, books, notions, and paper outlets, plus a few food and entertainment venues. Open from Monday–Saturday 9 a.m.–9 p.m. and from 9 a.m.–7 p.m. on Sunday, this mall is small enough to take in even when your feet are tired. Arranged in a rough circle, no shop of the approximately forty there is invisible or very distant. Call (800) SHOP-USA for specific information or explore their internet site at http://factorystores.com.

Across Hwy. 76 from Andy Williams theater, the **Tanger Outlet Center** promises "Guilt-Free Shopping" (if you can imagine that) in its approximately 60 shops with more planned for the future. Part of a national chain with 25 other outlets, you can find out more at the internet site: http://www. tangeroutlet.com. In Branson, upscale apparel outlets such as Tommy Hilfiger, Liz Claiborne, and Polo Ralph Lauren co-exist in the rectangle with Mikasa housewares and Arnold Palmer's Golf Store. A quadrangle set at the bottom of a hill, your best bet is a drive down to it. Open seven days, but call to confirm the hours of operation. (417) 337-9327 or (800) 4-TANGER.

The **Engler Block,** on 76 at the east end of the Strip near 65, is an enclosed artisan grouping of about 30 stores with some demonstration crafts such as glass-blowing and dulcimer-making. The **Branson Mall on 76,** where the Wal-Mart is, also includes an Ernest Tubb Record Store and various smaller shops. There are also a series of small shopping clusters, primarily crafts but with some clothing, on Highway 165 in and around the Branson Towne Theatre.

Part Nine

Outdoor Recreation

The Great Outdoors

We assume that most of you reading this book are primarily interested in Branson as an entertainment site, so we have emphasized the theaters, traffic tips, and lodging options. However, most of us at the *Unofficial Guides* happen to be interested in athletics and outdoor sports, and tend to mix a little exercise into even our busiest trips away from home, so we at least took a quick look around.

Because of the topography and the traffic, there is limited opportunity for joggers or bikers to enjoy their sports in Branson itself. However, if you're willing to drive a few miles—or if you're camping in one of the state parks—you'll find some pretty trails. There are a half-dozen golf courses in the Branson vicinity—golf is probably the second most popular sport in the area—and public tennis courts in downtown Branson along the waterfront park. The numbers for the golf courses are below; no reservations are needed for the tennis courts.

The vast majority of the sports facilities in the area have to do with the water: fishing, boating, skiing, sailing, parasailing, etc. Fishing is foremost, and we've included some information on the fish and where they're most apt to bite, where to rent equipment if you don't have it, etc. Boating and water safety regulations, along with information on fishing and the Missouri Wildlife Code, are available from the Branson/Lakes Chamber of Commerce, (417) 334-4136. Fishing licenses, both seasonal and short-term, are available at the Wal-Mart and many liquor and convenience stores in Branson. Trout anglers need a Missouri Trout Stamp as well as a fishing license for fishing in Lake Taneycomo. Several of the marinas listed below also offer instruction in water sports, too; call individual marinas for more information.

Incidentally, if you are interested in fishing the area lakes, you should plan to visit the Bass Pro Outdoor World complex in Springfield, a self-enclosed mega-mall of sporting goods shops and customizers complete with indoor waterfall and lagoon, seven-foot polar bears for photo souvenirs, hunting museum, and a huge overlook restaurant called Hemingway's, whose bar wall is a vast aquarium stocked with exotic species. Call Bass Pro Outdoor World at (417) 887-7334 or the Springfield Convention and Visitors Bureau at (800) 678-8766 for more information.

FISH STORIES

Branson is also referred to as the Tri-Lakes District because the three lakes (Bull Shoals, Lake Taneycomo, and Table Rock Lake) that *were* the White River run from east to west right through Branson and beyond. Bull Shoals is the farthest east, beyond the Powersite Dam near Forsythe; Lake Taneycomo is between the two dams (it is the stretch of "riverfront" visible in downtown Branson); and Table Rock Lake is west of town below Table Rock Dam.

In the beginning, the White River was one of the region's best-known fishing and camping sites. When the Powersite Dam was completed in 1913, it created Lake Taneycomo but it remained a warm-water site, popular for bass and panfish. Not until Table Rock Dam was completed in 1958 did the lake water turn cold, fed from the bottom of the power pool at Table Rock; now, with the assistance of the Shepherd of the Hills trout hatchery alongside, Lake Taneycomo is a trout bonanza. More than 800,000 trout are taken from the lake every year. Record catches include a 15 lb., 6 oz. white sucker and a 23 lb., 4 oz. German brown trout. Because of the stocking program, fishing is a strong year-round draw.

There is good fly-fishing in the Lake Taneycomo headwaters, especially in the first mile below the dam; after that, the old river bluffs make wading problematic. Fly rods, jigs (especially shrimp-shaped ones), and small bobbers are widely used, along with some drift- and worm-fishing from the accessible banks. In the wider lower water, boat fishing predominates. Even farther down the river (people still speak of it as a river, and it looks like one, since the two dams are 22 miles apart) is the old Downtown Branson waterfront, with a park area, public fishing docks, picnicking, tennis courts, a baseball diamond, and a city pool. This is also the area that the *Sammy Lane* Pirate Cruises, *Lake Queen,* and *Princess* leave from.

Below the town—this is actually northeast of town, but "downriver"— the bluffs rise again, the water is slightly warmer and more crappie and bluefish mix with the bass; below that is the town of Rockaway Beach, with its own Main Street, waterfront park, restaurants, and pavilion, once a big-band stop on the Kansas City and St. Louis circuit. Rockaway Beach, like Table Rock State Park, is a water sports center, with paddleboats, canoes, and pontoons; but below that the fishing is good again down to the dam, with catfish, crappie, and panfish along with the bass.

Bull Shoals Lake, east of the Powersite Dam beyond Forsythe, is less developed than either Table Rock or Taneycomo, and is well-stocked with black, largemouth, smallmouth, and spotted bass, walleyes, crappies, and white and striped bass. It is the site of several tournaments.

Sawtoothed Table Rock Lake has nearly 750 miles of shoreline, deep channels, and a feisty bass population, primarily largemouth, smallmouth, and Kentucky bass, along with crappie, catfish, and bluegill. Spring and late fall are the best time for fishing here, but summer and even the warmer stretches of winter are productive.

Table Rock Lake Marinas and Boat Docks

A variety of jet-ski, scuba, pontoon, bass boat, and fishing equipment are available for rent and occasionally purchase. Some marinas have fishing guides and scuba or parasailing instructors on staff as well. Call individual marinas for hours, equipment, and other specific information. Remember that many of the camping and condo resorts also have private marinas as well.

Cape Fair Boat Dock   Lake Road 76-82; (417) 538-4163.

Coombs Ferry   Highway JJ north of 86 (launching ramp only).

Cow Creek   Lake Road 86-10, southwest of Branson off 86.

Cricket Creek Marina   Highway 14 west off US 65.

Gage's Long Creek Marina   Lake Road 86-50, south of Branson off 86; (417) 334-4860.

Indian Point Boat Dock   Indian Point Road just off 76, south of Silver Dollar City; (417) 338-2891.

Old Highway 86 area   Off Highway UU on the northwest side of the Highway 86 lake bridge.

Port of Kimberling   Highway 13 in Kimberling City.

Table Rock State Park   One mile south of Table Rock Dam off 165/265; (417) 334-3069.

Lake Taneycomo Marinas and Boat Docks

The commercial and public-use areas at Lake Taneycomo are more specifically fishing-oriented. Call individual marinas for hours, equipment and other specific information. Remember that most camping and condo resorts also have private marinas as well. For more information call the Rockaway Beach information line at (800) 798-0178.

Fish Camp Marina   200 W. Beach Boulevard, Rockaway Beach; (417) 561-4213.

Taneycomo Marina   1101 Beach Boulevard, Rockaway Beach; (417) 561-8225.

HIKING AND OFF-ROAD TRAILS

For specific directions, use restrictions, and trail length, contact these parks directly.

Ruth and Paul Henning State Conservation Area   Highway 76 about a mile north of Branson. Call (417) 334-3324.

Dewey Shot Visitors Center   On 165 just south of Table Rock Dam. Call (417) 334-4704.

Mark Twain National Forest and Hercules Glade Wilderness Area (various trails)   Tower Trailhead is on Highway 125 eight miles south of 76 (from an intersection one mile east of Bradleyville); Coy Bald trailhead is on a marked gravel road 3 miles north of US 160 (from an intersection 6 miles east of Forsythe). Call (417) 683-4428.

Table Rock State Park   Off Highway 165/265 a mile below Table Rock Dam. Call (417) 334-4104.

Also: Glade Top Trail, along Forest Service Road No. 147 southeast of Brown Branch; Busiek State Forest, Highway 65, 15 miles north of Branson; Drury-Mincy Conservation Area, Highway 76, 6 miles east of Branson.

GOLF COURSES

For more information, directions, and tee times, and reservations, call the course directly.

Holiday Hills Resort & Golf Course

Address   630 East Rockford Drive, Branson, MO 65616

Phone   (417) 334-4838

Status   Semiprivate course

Tees   Men's: 5,771 yards, par 68.
Ladies': 4,414 yards, par 68.

Fees   Greens fee: $61 for 18 holes; $37 for 9 holes.

Facilities   Pro shop and restaurant.

Comments   May call up to three days ahead to reserve tee times. Open Tuesday through Saturday, 9 a.m.–4 p.m.

Kimberling Hills Country Club

Established   1967

Address   1 Lakeshore Drive, Kimberling City, MO 65686

Phone   (417) 739-4370

Status   Semiprivate course

Tees   Men's: 2,469 yards, par 34, slope 118.
Ladies': 2,360 yards, par 36, slope 131.

Fees   Greens fee: $11 for 9 holes. Cart fee: $6 per person.

Facilities   Pro shop, putting green, snack bar, lounge, banquet facilities.

Oakmont Community Golf Course

Established   1987

Address   2722 Highway 86, Ridgedale, MO (10 miles south of Branson)

Phone   (417) 334-1572

Status   Public course

Tees   Men's: 2,939 yards, par 36.
Ladies': 2,408 yards, par 36.

Fees   Greens fee: $17 for 18 holes; $12 for 9 holes. Cart fee: $12 for each 9 holes.

Facilities   Pro shop and limited snack bar.

Thousand Hills Golf Club

Established   1995

Address   245 South Wildwood Drive, Branson, MO 65616

Phone   (417) 334-4553

Status   Public course

Tees   Championship: 5,111 yards, par 64.
Men's: 4,439 yards, par 64.
Ladies': 3,616 yards, par 64.

Fees   Greens fee: $59 for 18 holes (includes cart fee); $35 for 9 holes (includes cart fee).

Facilities   Pro shop, club house, snack tent, restaurant, and meeting and group facilities.

Unofficial Guide **Reader Survey**

If you would like to express your opinion about Branson or this guide-book, complete the following survey and mail it to:

> *Unofficial Guide* Reader Survey
> PO Box 43673
> Birmingham AL 35243

Inclusive dates of your visit: _____

*Members of
your party:*   Person 1   Person 2   Person 3   Person 4   Person 5

Gender: M F   M F   M F   M F   M F

Age: _____

How many times have you been to Branson?   _____
On your most recent trip, where did you stay?   _____

Concerning your accommodations, on a scale of 100 as best and 0 as worst, how would you rate:

The quality of your room?   _____   The value of your room?   _____
The quietness of your room? _____   Check-in/check-out efficiency? _____
Swimming pool facilities?   _____

Did you rent a car? _____ From whom? _____

Concerning your rental car, on a scale of 100 as best and 0 as worst, how would you rate:

Pick-up processing efficiency? _____   Return processing efficiency? _____
Condition of the car?   _____   Cleanliness of the car?   _____
Airport shuttle efficiency?   _____

Concerning your dining experiences:

Including fast-food, estimate your meals in restaurants per day? _____
Approximately how much did your party spend on meals per day? _____
Favorite restaurants in Branson: _____

_____

Did you buy this guide before leaving? ☐   while on your trip? ☐

How did you hear about this guide? (check all that apply)

Loaned or recommended by a friend ☐   Radio or TV ☐
Newspaper or magazine ☐   Bookstore salesperson ☐
Just picked it out on my own ☐   Library ☐
Internet ☐

✂

What other guidebooks did you use on this trip? _____

_____

_____

_____

On a scale of 100 as best and 0 as worst, how would you rate them?

_____

_____

_____

Using the same scale, how would you rate *The Unofficial Guide(s)?*

_____

Are *Unofficial Guides* readily available at bookstores in your area? _____

Have you used other *Unofficial Guides?* _____

Which one(s)? _____

_____

_____

_____

_____

Comments about your Branson trip or *The Unofficial Guide(s):*

_____

_____

_____

_____

_____

_____

_____

_____

_____

_____

_____

_____

_____